*"Everyday Adventures* is filled with sweet, simple, everyday wisdom. It guides us to see all of life as a meditation and a gift. Each chapter invites us to pause and reflect with easy daily practices that deepen our experience of the ordinary. We are reminded that the simplest aspects of life can contain its greatest learnings and pleasures. It will open your eyes and your heart."

—Jett Psaris, Ph.D. & Marlena S. Lyons, Ph.D., authors of *Undefended Love*

*"Everyday Adventures for the Soul* offers an engaging, imaginative, delightful, and deep way for everyone to have a spiritual adventure a week!"

—Laurie Beth Jones, author of *Jesus CEO* and *The Path*

D1372056

# everyday adventures
## for the *Soul*

52 Simple &

Surprising Ways

to Wow Your Spirit

JUELI GASTWIRTH & AVRAM DAVIS, PH.D.

New Harbinger Publications, Inc.

*Publisher's Note*

*This publication is designed to provide accurate and authoritative information in regard to the subject matter covered. It is sold with the understanding that the publisher is not engaged in rendering psychological, financial, legal, or other professional services. If expert assistance or counseling is needed, the services of a competent professional should be sought.*

Distributed in the U.S.A. by Publishers Group West; in Canada by Raincoast Books; in Great Britain by Hi Marketing, Ltd.; in South Africa by Real Books, Ltd.; in Australia by Boobook; and in New Zealand by Tandem Press.

Cover design by Amy Shoup
Edited by Mike Ashby
Text design by Michele Waters

ISBN 1-57224-298-1 Paperback

New Harbinger Publications' Web site address: www.newharbinger.com

04    03    02

10    9    8    7    6    5    4    3    2    1

First printing

*To my mother and father.*
*And to the holy SPARK in each of us.*

—Jueli Gastwirth


*To my family, who have always tried to help me hear the music.*

—Avram Davis, Ph.D.

# Contents

# Introduction

*Everyday Adventures for the Soul* is filled with small everyday suggestions on how to simply tap into the world of spirituality. It is written for every person yearning for more spirit, but especially for those who look to the world as their sacred cathedral and not toward any particular religion or dogma. In truth, spirituality doesn't require a lot of time or tradition—it simply requires a yearning for connection, an eager awareness, and an open heart. It asks that you be patient with yourself, that you keep in the forefront of your mind the well-being of others, and that you know—in your heart of hearts—that enjoying yourself is just as spiritual as a long litany of dharma.

These stories and teachings are written with the idea that philosophy is not always a surefire guide to connection, but that simple deeds and stories are the very heart of the universe. Indeed, the universe consists of both.

People seek and yearn. But our ultimate yearning is answered only by the very simple. It is answered not by additional wealth (though a bit more salary never hurt!), or additional professional power, or by unnecessary sacrifice, or unreasonable commitment. Ultimately, yearning is answered only by a transformation that naturally occurs in our deepest self. When we embrace that transformation, we begin to act, see, and hear with the body, eyes, and ears of the heart and not just with the body, eyes, and ears of the flesh.

If you look with an open heart at the unfolding miracle of your own story and the rushing cascade of the stories of people around you, you are sure to be enriched on every level of being.

It's simpler than you imagine to deepen your spiritual relationship with yourself, with those you love, with the environment, and, ultimately, with the deepest source of connection. May these words serve, in some small way, to open the channel between your innermost heart and your activities in the world. May they help you to embody your thoughts, feelings, actions, and presence in the exact way you've always craved they could be.

Having fun and staying aware are the first steps to all that follows.

---

PART I

*Think It*

# Twist toward Abundance

How many times have you seen a penny on the ground and ignored it? Every time you see money on the ground—even if it's only a copper penny—it signals abundance. Money is practically falling from the sky and landing at your feet! The next time you see money on the ground, pick it up, put it in your pocket, and say to yourself or aloud, "Thanks for the abundance in my life." That simple statement acknowledges life's unceasing flow of generosity, and signals to the universe that you're aware of, thankful for, and ready for more abundance, always.

Abundance can be that simple. Especially in America, there are more options, more decisions, and more opportunities because of the overflowing abundance available to you in every minute, in every choice. It's almost overwhelming. As you'll see in Danni's story, however, it's a matter of how you respond that dictates abundant flow or its lack.

Danni was an avid hiker. She lived near a five-thousand-acre park and walked in it with her dog, Tora, nearly every day. Friends would join her to walk and talk, breathing fresh air while discussing the modern-day challenges and opportunities of their everyday lives. Staying physically hydrated was a priority.

Danni had been eyeing a deluxe water pack for nearly two seasons. Her budget was limited, though. So she saved; and as spring's emerald green hills turned to fall's wheat-colored grasses, Danni finally had enough money to buy a deluxe water pack of her own.

She felt excited as she stepped into the camping store. She only had twenty minutes to purchase the bottle, as she was on her way to an important meeting. Rushing into the store, Danni immediately was overcome with abundance.

More than fifty varieties of the water pack were available; each was designed for a myriad of distinct situations. Danni's reaction could have been one of many: she could have been overwhelmed by the many choices and her limited time; she could have been disgusted by her country's consumerism and material waste; she

4

could have been saddened by her financial limitations. To Danni's credit, she delighted in the freedom of choice available to her.

Whether you believe you have too little or too much, it remains true that your options always are abundant. The sense of abundance allows you to see and make choices based on what you want, regardless of whether true abundance is obvious. For example, if you don't have a lot of money, there are always less expensive options. If you have physical challenges but still want to be outside and active, there are choices. Abundance allows you to do whatever you want, as long as you can identify it. And that, without doubt, can take some practice.

Here's an exercise that will help you twist your thinking toward abundance, and, as a result, experience more calm, more peace, and more opportunities.

Here's what you can do:

1. The next time you're in a situation that causes you an emotionally charged response, recognize that charge as a beacon of opportunity and abundance. Take three deep breaths: inhale through your nose, exhale through your mouth.

2. Then, locate the choice you have before you by identifying and naming the opportunity of abundance of your situation.

Begin with identifying abundance in positive situations, as it's easier to recognize abundance in a pay raise, or a declaration of love, or a physical accomplishment. Don't wait too long, however, to identify and name the abundance in supposedly negative situations. Whether you're feeling overwhelmed or frightened or nervous or angry—there is abundance and opportunity in those situations as well. If you're unemployed, for example, you have an abundance of choices of what to do with your day. If you're not feeling well, you have the choice to relax, to watch movies, to sit in the sun. Every option, every choice, every situation can be seen through a lens of abundance. Search for, identify, and embrace your options. They're abundant. Try it and see.

# Falling Down and Getting Up

Getting up is hard. Each of us, buffeted by the failures and tragedies that have defined major parts of our lives, has learned (usually after great pain) the danger of getting up too quickly after we have fallen or been knocked down. Getting up is hard. Every one of us has been down on the ground, looking up (even if metaphorically) and knowing in our bones the likelihood of the pain repeating itself if we got up and reentered the fray. For most of us, this has been a hard-won knowledge and deeply ingrained perspective.

Usually such perspectives are good to pay attention to. Precisely because they have been acquired through difficulty and travail, they mean something to us. Usually they are some form of defense—a defense that has helped us, so we continue to use it.

Just because something has been good for us in the past, however, does not ensure its usefulness in the present or the future. It is equally important to pay attention to our present mental and spiritual condition in order to weigh the possibility that we have outgrown some of our old patterns and that perhaps some of the deeply drawn grooves in our behavior have become destructive ruts. Almost every defensive behavior of our past eventually becomes a destructive rut and demands that we change it. It is a precious voice, whenever it makes itself heard.

Think a moment. You were not always so hesitant about trying new things and getting involved and re-involved with whatever was going on around you. For example, for most of us, childhood was a time of great exploration and discovery. That childlike way of being (notice, though, this does not mean childish) is the natural legacy of being human. We are never meant to lose it. The creation of new experience and new ways in which to interact with the experience are one of the most precious gifts of higher consciousness.

Margie took Mary, her young daughter, to the playground. She watched as Mary bounced around, curious about everything and getting into everything. Every moment or two her bright, young voice would call out: "Look Mama, look at this!" —a snail on a leaf. "Look Mama, come over here!" she squealed—a dandelion flower stood like a tiny white umbrella among the green grasses. At first, Margie was patient and went over every time to inspect what her daughter was doing. Then she began to feel the first stirring of annoyance. "Good grief," she thought, "it's just a dandelion." Then she was granted an insight of grace and realized none of what her daughter saw or did was *just* anything. Each thing Mary saw was an insight into an entirely different way of being in the world. She was not concerned with the potential for failure. She was not concerned with the potential for pain. She was seeing each thing just as itself. And each thing was simply extraordinary.

In such matters it was Mary who was the teacher, not Margie. And Margie thought of the truth spoken from the wisdom of a child, and she suddenly saw a different way of seeing.

For to Mary, every blade of grass was an entire world for her to explore. With bursts of energetic joy she bounded across the field toward her next exploration. Unfortunately she could not bound very well. In truth, she hadn't been walking all that long. And after a step or two she would fall on her face. But immediately she would rise again, usually with a smile on her face, and resume her quest—unless she was diverted by some new bright interest that beckoned her.

"Baby, are you okay?" Margie called. Mary laughed and bounded off.

We carry the potential of each of our ages with us. We carry the history of our whole life with every step we make in the world. The next time you see children playing, pause for a moment and watch them. Or, if you have the time, spend an hour or two at a playground observing. Perhaps take a sketchbook and sketch their energetic play, including a few words describing what you are seeing. At the least, let your mind drift and be in that space, if only for a few moments. Let it impact your day. Ask yourself who you would be with that level of play and ability to fall down, laugh, and get up and keep running.

# I Love You to Life

"Watch what you say!" shouldn't be just an old adage floating around in your head from early childhood days. When your mother taught you to be polite by minding your word choice, she was also teaching you "word awareness," one of the most helpful, life-affirming mindfulness tools you'll ever acquire.

Word awareness means exactly what it sounds like: being attentive and alert to the words you use. Some words spread through your heart like drops of honey; some leave a strand of negativity coiling through your system for days. With word awareness, you alter your subconscious into a honeycomb rather than a trash receptacle.

Being aware of your words is challenging, but it's essential. Studies have proven time and again that negative words create negative images, which negatively affect your health. Imagine, for example, how continually talking about death affects how you feel. Do you think it would make you feel more vibrant, alive, and physically fit, or do you think it would pull you down a bit, both emotionally and physically?

Take a look at the following lists. As you read through the common clichés in the left column, make a mental note as to how many of them you use or hear without thinking of what the word "death" *actually* means and/or how it affects you. Just for fun, the column to the right is a list of comparable but more life-affirming alternatives you may want to try speaking instead.

| Common Death Clichés | Alternatives |
| --- | --- |
| Laughing to death | Laughing to life |
| Crying to death | Crying to life |
| To die for | To live for |
| Deadline | Time line |
| Dead serious | Very serious |

| | |
|---|---|
| I love you to death | I love you to life |
| I'm dying to do that | I'm living to do that |

It's amazing, but word awareness, and hence the effects it has on your health, can be as simple as changing your focus from cliché speaking to conscious word choice. For example, exchanging the word "life" in the clichés above with the word "death" is bound to affect you. And others certainly will take note of it as well.

Kate, a young up-and-coming film director from New York, was finishing up a three-month across-the-country road trip filming a documentary about bars, trailer parks, and side-street alleys across America. It had only been a few months since she'd last seen her mom, but Kate was glad to be home just the same.

Kate decided to clean up before having dinner. With water jetting against her back in the shower and a bucketful of suds atop her head, Kate heard her mom open the bathroom door and shout in to her:

"Oh, honey, I just love you to death!"

Based on years of paying close attention to movie dialogue, Kate found her mother's word choice odd. Kate was the happiest she could remember being in years: she was in good health, visiting her mom, filming a documentary, traveling across the country. In this joy-filled time, how odd it was to think about her life coming to an end; to think about dying.

All these thoughts happened in a flash, and Kate smiled. Ultimately, she knew her mom was just being loving. Kate laughed at the absurdity, opened the glass shower door, and yelled to her mother across the house, "I love you to LIFE, Ma. I love you to life."

It isn't difficult to stay aware of your words, but it does take some attention. Just remember, the words of your favorite author, poet, or politician may deeply move you, and words spoken by your mother or your spouse certainly have their own unique effects—but generally speaking, the words you say yourself are most poignant of all.

---

# The Art of Could Be

Everyone gets into trouble. It's part of being human. Indeed, it may be a direct consequence of having a mind—not so much the getting into trouble, but the way people have of going out looking for trouble. Growing up, most people have a fair share of searching out mischief and trouble of one sort or another.

Stanley's dad had a couple of favorite stories that he would bring forth whenever Stanley, as a youngster, got in a situation he figured was hopeless. One of them went like this. Once there was a king whose chief adviser displeased him and he sentenced him to die. Quick-witted, the adviser said, "Don't kill me, King, because I know a great secret. I can make a wooden horse fly." Immediately the king had his son's wooden horse brought.

"Oh King," said the adviser. "It is not so simple as that. I cannot do it in just a moment. Allow me to live and within one year I will make that horse fly. If I fail, I will offer my life." He said this very sincerely. The king, feeling suspicious, looked at him a long time. Finally he shrugged. "All right," he said. "Let it be done as you have asked." Why not, he thought. What did he have to lose?

Later that evening friends of the adviser came to visit him. "What are you doing?" they said. "You know there is no way you can succeed." They shook their heads over the folly, or perhaps insanity, of their friend. He laughed. "You think me mad, my friends, but it is not so. Think a moment. A great deal can change in one year. Maybe the king will die. Perhaps there will be a revolution, and maybe, just maybe, I'll make that darned horse fly!"

A lot of problems come to people from their difficulty in imagining. They see the evil in the world and just can't believe there is a God of good, or a force of redemption, or a silver lining in whatever cloud is casting its shadow at the moment. The weight of difficulty seems too great and the forces aligned against them too powerful. It does no good to tell them otherwise, because otherwise just sounds like Pollyannaish claptrap.

When we are in the midst of pain and suffering, it's pointless for others to speak of mercy, or give sage advice about how things are for the best, or even that it will definitely get better. Because, who knows? Perhaps it will, perhaps it won't. It is not in our ability or scope to know these kinds of answers in any definitive way.

So here comes the magical formula of *could be.* It's more powerful than any abracadabra. It permits the mind to avoid making a definite negative decision in the moment. Because the worst thing about fear, anger, and despair is that they seem unchangeable. Once in those states, we feel they'll last forever.

For example: Perhaps you get fired from your job and you fall into despair. If you tell yourself it's going to be all right, it's hard to believe yourself. Life just seems too miserable and dead-end. But you could tell yourself it's *possible* that something good could come from this; it *could be* that a new road will open up that will be better than the last one; why, it *could be.*

It is powerful to operate from the place of could be. The place of could be opens a lot of doors. It permits us to see that change is always happening, and we are part of the process of this change. The practice of could be is a powerful tool of insight and opened imagination. Try it. Take the afternoon and go for a walk. In each of the situations and scenes you see, apply the could be rule. You see people fighting and think: "It *could be* that fighting is not inevitable between people. Probable, yes, but it's not inevitable. Could be. It *could be* that people can live in peace. Could be. It could be that I can rise higher than I am, that I can hear the angels of my better nature more easily than I do."

Difficult? Yes. But, *could be.*

# Energy Follows Thought

Energy follows thought. That is, what you think greatly influences the reality of your experiences. Most everyone knows at least one person who tends to be more negative than positive; and some individuals, no matter what, always seem to be a bit on the happier side. The difference in these dispositions has little to do with actual experiences, and a whole lot to do with how each perceives the situations they're experiencing. (No blame here, but everyone can change!)

It isn't necessary to seek out life's pain and strife and struggle—these experiences come to everybody without having to go in search of them. One of life's challenges, instead, is to celebrate life: to focus on and to seek out the opportunity that each of us can access in all experiences. Dr. Viktor Frankl wrote extensively about his five years of imprisonment in Auschwitz and other concentration camps and his struggle during that time to find reasons to live. He describes in *The Meaning of Life* how he witnessed numerous individuals dancing and praying aloud as they were ushered into the gas chambers to die.

Admittedly, it's difficult to imagine dancing toward death, especially under such devastating circumstances. Still, as human beings we each individually determine the lens through which we filter our experiences, and, hence, how we spend our energy. Each of us personally decides to focus our attention positively or negatively as each situation unfolds.

The idea isn't simple, but it's true. And although, in some instances, it is imperative, or inescapable, to feel and experience the negative effects of a situation—it just as often is unnecessary to do so.

How many times, for instance, have you gawked at a fatal roadside accident while you were still emotionally bubbling inside from the frustration you felt for the past four miles of congested, bumper-to-bumper traffic? Instead of focusing your energy on negative thoughts, such as how late you're going to be to your appointment, how much you hate living in a city with congested traffic, and so on, train yourself to think positively (at the very least, your blood pressure will benefit).

For example, why not send positive healing thoughts of love and compassion for the family members, friends, and individuals who are directly involved with the accident? Or, roll down your window, cock your head to the side, and admire all the details of the scenery you never have a chance to admire at sixty-five miles per hour. Or, just smile at the person sitting in the car next to you. You get the idea.

Situations similar to these continually surround you. And the more you develop the ability to recognize and acknowledge the positive, the more enhanced your energy and outlook will become.

**Here's what you can do:** In a moment of frustration or negativity, take a breath and mentally interrupt your antagonistic thoughts. Acknowledge they exist, and then immediately choose to focus your energy on more positive, supportive, or relaxing ideas. For example:

❖ When the power goes out, appreciate a moment of respite in the wake of no electricity.

❖ When someone is late to meet you, be thankful for the newly found extra few minutes to finish up a household task you've been meaning to accomplish.

❖ When a loved one or business associate is raising her voice, mentally acknowledge the calmness or balance she'll soon feel after her emotional outburst.

A small shift in your awareness will open your eyes and your heart to more positive angles. Most definitely, it isn't always simple, and, sometimes, it feels downright impossible. Take a breath and seek out the benefits of your situation. You'll appreciate it more, positively.

# It's a Matter of Perception

How you experience and live within your day-to-day activities is a choice. Your reactions ultimately are based on how you choose to perceive situations. Each experience in and of itself does not hold a charge. Instead, the emotional impact of a situation depends on how you choose to see and engage with it. In the best of circumstances, you have the absolute ability to choose exactly how you respond to almost every experience. In more challenging situations, you at least can choose to respond in a manner that is most healthy for you and, ultimately, most balanced.

Before you can choose *how* you will react, however, you must first recognize that you *are* reacting. Then, after taking an extra breath or two, you can engage in a simple, spiritual practice: recognize the opportunity to choose awareness and compassion—for yourself and others.

- ❖ First, breathe. This means to consciously inhale and exhale, focusing exclusively on your breath.

- ❖ Second, recognize that regardless of how you have interpreted the situation at hand, there are at least ten thousand alternate explanations of the *how* and the *why* of it. Eventually these first two steps will take less than a minute, but initially they may require a bit more time and effort.

- ❖ Your next step is to choose a more balanced response. To do this, simply ask an open-ended question that will lead you toward compassion. For example, "How can I view this situation in a way that is not judgmental of me or the other person?" Or, "What perspective could they possibly be coming from that I'm not seeing?" Or, "How can I best respond from a place of openheartedness?"

- ❖ Then, breathe. And listen with your heart. Be open to humor, to the absurd, to the most ridiculous answers.

Although it was a big decision, Sara and John decided to spend the holidays with Sara's family, which meant traveling back east to the town where she grew up. When the holidays rolled around, Sara was delighted at how comfortable everybody was together: it seemed John had been coming home with her for years, and the usual tension between Sara and her brother, Ethan, seemed nowhere to be found.

After dinner, however, the situation changed dramatically. Ethan loudly and sarcastically began spouting his unsolicited opinions about Sara's reasons for moving to the West Coast, and, before long, the two were in a screaming match reminiscent of their childhood. It was a bit awkward for John, who tried to supportively intervene, hoping to bring calm to Sara. However, instead of feeling supported, Sara jumped to the reactive assumption that John had sided against her, and the loving words he chose to speak received a backlash of lifetime resentment.

Sara couldn't believe John had agreed with Ethan's outlandish and disrespectful comments. She felt so betrayed by both of them that it took her almost an entire day to calm down. Finally, when she had caught her breath, she asked herself: "What perspective could John possibly be coming from that I'm not seeing?" Remaining open, Sara took a few more deep breaths, and the myriad of possibilities began to trickle through her consciousness. Maybe she had misunderstood his comments in the flurry of emotion. Maybe he was actually being supportive. Maybe when he told her to stop shouting he was hoping to jar her out of her reactive state.

By recognizing these other possibilities, Sara was able to approach John openheartedly, taking responsibility for her behavior and feelings while remaining open and curious about what his experience had been.

Perspective can be a funny thing. When you're looking at the world through your eyes, everything makes sense; it's clear and absolute. Yet, the prescription of the personal lenses through which you look at the world is uniquely your own. It is refreshing to be curious about how others view the world. It's invaluable, however, to appreciate the validity of these different points of view and to know that it is from these differences that you learn most about yourself.

# You're Never Late

Everyone was rushing. The traffic was horrible, the weather miserable; sleet and rain made driving a nightmare. It was the kind of evening one should just stay home, but that was not an option for Jake. As he traveled, he found his mood going from neutral to angry overdrive with every mile. To top it all off, he got lost, couldn't find his map, had to get out in the pouring rain and ask directions from filling station clerks and convenience store cashiers.

When Jake finally turned into the driveway of the conference center, he was feeling on edge. In fact, he was feeling downright surly toward the world. As he jerked his bags out of the car and headed toward the registration entrance, a sign over the door arrested his progress. It was plainly painted, but might as well have been in neon.

It read: "You are not late."

It was a simple statement but it stopped him in his tracks. He looked at the sign for a few moments and began to chuckle as he contemplated the single sentence. "You are not late." He mulled it over and smiled. He thought, "Well of course, what could I be late for?"

The sign was a reminder, and it did its job very well. It reminded him that he was not really going anywhere. That he was only here, in this life for the weekend, so to speak. Wherever he was, he was. He was not late, regardless of what other people might think. When he entered the building, he walked over to the desk and thanked the people there for the reminder. A woman at the desk smiled. "Almost every single person who has arrived has thanked us for it," she said. "It seems everyone feels the burden of being late. It's chronic."

For Jake, the phrase "You are not late" became the theme for the entire weekend. It was what he thought about as he walked through the snowy woods, as he sipped his morning tea, and as he participated in the weekend workshops. There were several classes, some of them academic in tone, dealing with the nature of the mind; some of them experiential, helping people recognize their inner selves. But for Jake, the great insight of the weekend was formed during the first moment of getting to the conference.

Everyone works on a tight schedule. It is an American thing to do. Everyone feels the need to be at a certain place at a certain time. The work is rushed, the job is rushed, the boss is rushed. The baby is rushed to eat its food. The world is rushed to get to where it's going. But where are we all going?

In the larger sense, what is a person late for? Our life is just what we live. If we live it rushed, we have deprived ourselves of the great possibility of peace. Ultimately, for 99 percent of events, when we get there, that's when they start. But harassing ourselves about schedules just makes us neurotic. Arriving to a place is part of the process of the experience. Often it is the most important part of the experience, so it is important to be aware and astute regarding this.

An exercise to illustrate this is taking a cue from Jake's conference center experience: make yourself a simple sign, "You Are Not Late." Write this as a sign and reminder and tack it up somewhere in your house for a few days. Look at it periodically and repeat the teaching. Then take it down. After a few more days, put it back up again. Keep it up long enough to keep it fresh, but when you begin to ignore it, take it down for a little while. Try to do this for a couple of weeks. Put up a smaller version on the dashboard of your car. Hang it up at your favorite coffee shop. You will be tickled by the response, both within your own heart and from the people who notice it. We all work with this obstacle of mind, the cultural sense that we are always late. But for what exactly, we are usually hard-pressed to say.

If you keep this awareness for a while, you will notice that you begin to slow down and notice things a little differently. You will interact with people and situations in a different manner. Your heart will gradually become lighter and a subtle reprioritizing will happen. You will slowly start to become more human. You will not be late.

# Everything Means Something

Sometimes it's nearly impossible to know what you should do. It doesn't matter how much you think about, wish for, or want something, it's just plain difficult to know for sure which way to walk, what choices to make, or which decision is correct.

The truth is that you can learn to pay attention to life in a way that will unequivocally lead you step-by-step and in the most direct route possible toward your highest potential. Clear directions and signs are available everywhere, if only you learn to pay attention and heed their call.

The first step to developing this capacity is to have a clear idea about what it is you want to understand. When you have a topic of contemplation, put it into the form of a question. For example, if you were deciding whether you should buy a home or rent again, you would state your decision as, "I wonder whether I should purchase real estate this year or if I should live in another rental property."

Next, you must try to keep the question consciously in the forefront of your thoughts. One way to accomplish this is to write your question down on a piece of paper and place it somewhere that you can't avoid seeing and reading it at least once or twice a day. On your bathroom mirror, below your alarm clock, or on the car steering wheel are good locations to post your questions. Once you become more skilled at conscious attention, you can simply make a mental note that you're interested in learning about a certain question or direction you've been thinking of.

The next step is the trickiest: you have to pay attention to your day-to-day experiences so that you'll recognize the Universal signs as they come to you. You have to relate to your everyday interactions and encounters in a way that allows you to see what messages are being sent your way. You can think of this component as learning to "connect the dots."

To do this, you must learn to consciously discern how your question or topic interrelates with what you do during the day. For instance, if a For Sale sign is posted on your favorite house in the neighborhood the same day that you question whether to buy or rent a home, you'd inquire into the meaning of that. If you were inspired, you would call a real estate agent and take a look at the house. At the least, you would mentally explore what it might feel like if you purchased or lived in that home.

Once you note and follow through on a thought or idea related to your question, simply tuck away the information you gathered and continue with your day. It won't be long before another thought, sign, or idea will reveal yet another component of your question.

Suppose that later in the day you receive e-mail announcing that a colleague is being transferred to the company's overseas offices. Again, pay attention and then follow the dots. Would you want to live in the home your colleague will be vacating? At the most, you'd e-mail your business associate and ask how they're leaving their housing situation. At the least, you would wonder how you would feel living there.

When you approach your life as if you have an open-ended question that is interrelated to everything you see, do, and think, you begin to see guidance and signposts everywhere. Suddenly, the traffic that you're stuck in reminds you how much you dislike city congestion and moves you closer to the idea of changing locations; the morning newspaper headline sparks a connection to the entrepreneurial idea you had months ago and are now encouraged to reexamine; the conversation you overhear at your favorite coffeehouse triggers you to further explore the idea you had of attending a yoga retreat.

Not everything has to mean something, but it can. It just depends on how you choose to pay attention. Day by day, dot by dot, you can ask for and receive guidance about anything. Following the thread throughout your days most assuredly can lead you to where you're headed with the confidence that comes from doing exactly what feels right. Certainly you can succeed without enlisting the assistance of Universal signs, but why would you try to do so? Conscious living is fun, especially when you become good at it.

# Behind the Dalai Lama

Larry found himself behind a car that was making his blood boil. It all came down to this one car and, of course, he was stuck behind it. It was early Sunday morning, there was no football game happening, there was no real traffic about, but this one car would hardly move! It wasn't even going the speed limit. This sort of thing made Larry crazy. There was nowhere that he had to be especially, but he liked to move quickly.

In fact, moving quickly from place to place was a good metaphor for Larry's life. He liked to be in one place, then, if he needed to be somewhere else, he used some quick mode of conveyance to rapidly change locations. Sitting around in traffic, or in line, or in conversation was not his idea of anything good. He honked, but the driver just waved cheerily in the rearview mirror. The guy appeared to be wearing a robe. This made Larry even angrier. "The lane's free, and I'm behind a crazy guy in a robe," he thought. "Only in California. Why can't he put the pedal down?"

As if in answer, the car ahead seemed to slow down. (The road became a bit more curvy.) Mile after mile in a single lane with no traffic and yet no place to pull out, Larry was forced to follow a car going below the speed limit. "If this is a test of my patience," Larry thought, "I am surely failing."

He began to curse to himself, and thought: "Who does this guy think he is?" "What is he doing that is so important?" "He's not doing surgery in there!"

Finally there was a passing lane that opened and Larry floored the pedal. The car jumped forward as if it were newly released from a taut leash. As he came up even, window to window, with the car in front of him, he slowed down for a moment to look at the people in the car and perhaps give them a piece of his mind (or his finger).

As he looked through the glass, the first thing he noticed was that the car was crowded. The people in the car were short and Larry had not been able to see them from behind, though now he could make out that they were all wearing dresses.

"No," he corrected himself, "robes—they're all dressed in robes of some sort." As his mind absorbed this, he glanced into the backseat and into the eyes of the Dalai Lama. This fact took a good three seconds to register in his brain.

The Dalai Lama looked up from his work and saw Larry staring. He gently waved and smiled a big, tooth-filled smile at Larry's gaping, speechless face and then bent back to his work. This drew the attention of the other monks in the car (there seemed to be half a dozen at least), and they all started waving excitedly and saying things to Larry through the glass that he couldn't hear but would have sworn were: "Be happy!" "Enjoy this beautiful day." "How is your practice going?" punctuated by more happy waves and smiles.

In confusion, Larry let his foot off the gas and fell back behind the car again. The single lane reasserted itself, this time with concrete construction barriers that made passing out of the question, and they traveled together in this way several more miles at the same slow, measured rate.

But for Larry, there was quite a difference in attitude this time. For a long time he simply drove speechless and essentially thoughtless, his mind just forming the words: "The Dalai Lama? Yes, the Dalai Lama!"

We never know who we might be behind in traffic, or next to in line. That person buying carrots may have saved the lives of many, might be selfless and generous in a way that we have only dreamed of being. It is precious to think who that person might be. Certainly they are quite unique, never to be seen in their particular form again.

As an exercise, for a few days imagine that you are driving behind the Dalai Lama. Or in front of you at the store is St. Francis. Or Mother Teresa is on the street corner. Ask yourself, "Could the person holding that baby be St. Francis?" "Could the woman on the corner be Mother Teresa?" "Who am I driving behind—could it be the Dalai Lama?"

Indeed it could. Indeed, it almost certainly is.

# O the Moon

Before 1969, when humankind first set foot on the Moon, the Earth's illuminated satellite was somewhat of a mystery hovering in the sky. Since then, of course, we've learned a lot more about it; though, long before history lessons and astronomical information, the Moon's brilliant cyclical beauty was always present.

The glory and consistency of the Moon cycle affect us all. Since the beginning of time, the Moon has been a compass to the seasons, the months, and even the evening hours. Many Native American tribes, goddess traditions, and Middle Eastern people base their calendars on the thirteen-month cycle of the Moon. Some communities schedule rituals and celebrations based solely on the Moon cycle. Even people who rarely think of the Moon will stop and pause when the light of a rising full moon kisses their forehead in the night.

Each month, the Moon moves through a series of phases. The start of each cycle begins with the *new moon*, when the Moon's unilluminated side is facing the Earth. That means, when you look in the sky, the Moon is not visible (except during a solar eclipse). As the illumination of the Moon increases, we say the Moon is *waxing*. It waxes through the first *crescent moon* and the first *quarter moon*. When it passes the halfway mark of illumination, it is called a *gibbous moon*. It's a *full moon* when it appears completely illuminated in the sky. After it's full, illumination gradually decreases, which is referred to as *waning*. During this time, the Moon moves through each of its phases in reverse: gibbous, quarter, and crescent; then it begins again as new.

You could spend a lifetime learning all about the Moon and its phases, but the best way to truly enjoy its majestic qualities is to look up in the sky. Whichever phase the Moon is in, spend a few moments—or just a flicker of a moment if that's all you can spare—to marvel at its beauty or luminosity, or to wonder at its distance from the Earth. Be awed by its purity, by the fact that it has continued for millenniums to cycle in just the same way it is cycling today. Gaze at its color, or its location relative to the horizon and the stars. Stare at it for a second, and enjoy the gift of lunar respite.

Once you start looking for the Moon, you'll be surprised at how often you take note of it floating across the evening sky. Use the Moon and your awareness of it as a tool to stay conscious, present, and aware. Play with the meanings of its cycles and coordinate them with various areas and focuses of your life. Here are a few examples.

**New moon and/or first crescent moon:** When the sky is empty of the Moon or when just a sliver of it is illuminated, think of everything new in your life or anything you wish could be new. The new moon is an auspicious time to begin new projects, have new conversations, enjoy new experiences. It is a time for celebration; to recognize that a new cycle is beginning; to consciously state a few hopes or dreams or ideas you can explore or accomplish in the coming month. The new moon is also a great time to enjoy the night sky—the sparkle of the stars more dazzling in the absence of moonlight.

**Waxing or waning:** When you look into the sky and see the Moon, recognize its luminosity and try to guess if its glow is increasing (waxing) or slowly decreasing (waning). If it's waxing, think of what you'd like to gain more of; if it is waning, think of some items or personality traits you'd like to experience a little less of every day.

**Full moon:** When the Moon is beaming a full circle of light through the night sky, take an extra few moments to bask in its glow. Relate your life, your emotions, or your monthly experiences to the wholeness of the Moon's glow, to the stunning totality it emits, to the bedazzling entirety of its light. Find a seed of gratitude for those areas of your life where you feel complete, or for any circumstance for which you feel abundance, gratitude, or generosity. It can be an added bonus to metaphorically be light—more carefree—on the full moon. If you have the time, for instance, go outside and find your Moon shadow to play with, or read stories about the Moon to your children, or sleep outside with the stars as your roof.

However you choose to develop, to court, or to embrace your relationship with the Moon, do so soon, this month, during this Moon cycle. Don't wait for a blue moon before you introduce yourself. Go outside tonight and look up in the sky.

# Release, Forgive, and Let Go

Forgiveness often feels like it's about someone else. Someone at some time did something that hurt you, and, one day perhaps, you may find the desire, strength, or willingness to forgive him or her. The truth, however, is that forgiving others has as much to do with our own health and energy level as it does with anyone else's. Holding on to negativity will eat away at your own core as it simultaneously sends a negative current through the universe to the target of your grudge. When we truly release someone from the responsibility of causing us hurt, discomfort, pain, anguish, and so on—whether it's in the moment or whether it's years later—the release frees up a huge amount of personal energy and effort, and makes room for the new.

This doesn't discount deep wounds and pain that require therapy, deep compassion, and focused effort. For these types of injuries, of course, it is important to be tender and allow yourself the appropriate time to recover. But try to be honest with how you experience past pain and anguish: does it take more effort to stay connected with that person through your anger and/or hurt than it would to forgive and let go?

Patricia, a thirty-three-year-old interior designer, didn't quite know what hit her when she first met Andy, a carpenter from Rhode Island. What she experienced was exactly what she always imagined she'd feel when she finally met her soul companion. Between her good looks and his charm, the new lovebirds rapidly became inseparable. At first, neither Andy nor Patricia could do wrong.

In less than eight weeks, and quite unexpectedly, however, Andy declared the relationship a great mistake and disappeared without explanation from Patricia's day-to-day life. She was devastated, hurt, and confused.

Then, out of nowhere, just as quickly as Andy had appeared and disappeared, he reappeared asking for Patricia's forgiveness. (Was he crazy?) How could she possibly forgive him? A part of her wanted him to hurt as she had hurt. By letting go of the grudge, did it mean it was okay for him to have rejected her, causing her pain and confusion?

On some level, Patricia knew that by not forgiving Andy she was choosing to hold on to all of that pain and negativity—and on to a fantasy relationship long since expired. She took a deep breath. And smiled. And forgave. Not so surprisingly, she felt better. She no longer was giving her power away. She felt free of him and almost immediately felt better about herself and her availability to new, healthier relationships.

If you've done the hard work of healing but just can't seem to completely release, let go, and forgive, here are a few suggestions:

- ❖ Each time you think of the person, mentally send a positive thought their way. For example, imagine the person in your mind and then say aloud or to yourself, "I wish you peace and success in all your endeavors." It sounds goofy, but it really helps to release them.

- ❖ When you notice yourself thinking about the situation, wave your hand across your face, imagining that you are completely wiping the thought (and the person) from your mind.

- ❖ Write a letter expressing all of the hurt and anger you've felt, then write, ". . . for all of these things, I forgive you." Burn or shred the letter.

Certainly, not all situations are simple or easy. Many are emotionally overwhelming and their life lessons and gifts are most difficult to ascertain. Still, there comes a time in most of life's less complicated circumstances when you innately know that you needn't hang on anymore. It becomes clear that you've learned what you need to from the situation at hand. To create new space for new experiences and people, you must release—and forgive—from your heart completely.

# It's So Imperfect!

Unless you've lived in seclusion this past decade or two, you'd have to admit that the perfect, highly digitized world of computers has influenced your productivity and expectations. Although you appreciate the modern computer and all of the conveniences it allows, if you're like most Americans, the digital age has greatly affected how grand, how quick, and how perfect you expect your life, your tasks, and your accomplishments to be.

Amidst all the hubble-bubble of modern advancement, many people occasionally crave that the pendulum swing in the opposite direction: after spending eight hours (or more) a day coddling alphabet keys and manipulating high-tech mice, who hasn't driven home wishing for a more simple, imperfect, modest lifestyle? Can you imagine receiving accolades and promotions for being less than perfect? How would it be to feel accomplished in the fact that your latest project would remain forever incomplete?

Since the fifteenth century, the Japanese art of *wabi-sabi* has encouraged people to value things that are imperfect, impermanent, and incomplete. This elegant tradition perceives beauty in things that are flawed, worn, cracked, aged, torn, weathered, abandoned, or used. Although there is no direct English translation for the term *wabi-sabi*, it can be embraced within the Western idiom that "less is more"; it reveres the authentic; it apotheosizes nature. It's a philosophy. For instance, *wabi-sabi* is the single iris as opposed to a dozen red roses; it is the elegance of your grandmother's faded table covering versus a modern, sleek glass top; it is aesthetically appreciating your weathered old garage door, without a thought of repainting it.

*Wabi-sabi* is such a gift. An authentic, respected, and centuries-old tradition gives permission to appreciate and believe in those things that often, at least in the modern age, are viewed as unacceptable, degenerate, or less valuable.

To begin practicing the art of *wabi-sabi* simply:

❖ slow down your pace,

❖ quiet your mind, and

❖ identify the beauty in what already naturally exists.

*Wabi-sabi* is a mind-set more than anything. It's a way of being. It's an approach of appreciating yourself, others, and things, exactly as they are.

Living on a sailboat, Laurie learned to embrace and appreciate the art of *wabi-sabi:* her aging floorboards added character to her floating abode; the chipped mast told multiple tales of trips out to sea; in the cabin, only a select few niceties were displayed, as space allowed. Laurie loved the simplicity, the modesty, even the imperfection of living aboard the *Windsong.* Its flaws and limitations naturally led to her discovering an innate sense of inner peace and deep life appreciation.

After four years of floating, Laurie moved onto land. It didn't take long before she once again was involved with multiple *wabi-sabi* projects: she converted old doorways into tables, stitched beloved fabric into curtains, and painted the walls blue, a color that reminded her of the ocean, the sky, and of being outdoors.

When she finished painting the walls, Laurie knew she had practically become a *wabi-sabi* master. She painted for two days and then, as she rounded the corner, which was tucked between a closet and a doorway, she flung the brush aside in completion, leaving a small but significant section of the wall its natural color. To the Western eye, the paint job may have appeared incomplete, but to a seasoned *wabi-sabi* expert, it was perfect. The blue wall was lapping at the corner's whiteness, continually reminiscent of the ever-changing color permeations in the sky and the sea.

Finding beauty, meaning, and authenticity in the incomplete, the imperfect, and the impermanent is the heart of *wabi-sabi* and the essence of a more enjoyable lifestyle. The next time you catch yourself procrastinating so you can relax just a little bit longer, or you notice a chipped pot in your garden, or you grumble about mismatched dinnerware or clashing color coordination, think *wabi-sabi.* It's not an excuse; it's an art form. It's not about perfection; it's about appreciation.

# The Power of a Word

True power and true strength do not reside in iron or in an engine. True power resides in things that seem, at first glance, intangible. We are moved most deeply by the hidden rather than the obvious; but our deeper perceptions and feelings are often brought to a head by something very simple: a gesture, a moment, a piece of music, or a word.

Of all the invisible powers, few are greater or more transformative than the power of a word, said in the right moment. Each of us has had words spoken to us that we have carried with us our entire lives. We may forget, over time, the pain of a bone that was broken. But many of us remember a word spoken in anger for our whole lives. Words have shaped us, both toward the good and toward the ill.

Stanley got on the bus feeling pretty low. He had just lost his job. Although he didn't particularly like it, he needed it, and to top it off, his girlfriend had broken up with him the previous night. He was feeling bad.

As he sat down, he noticed an old man dressed in bib overalls sitting across the aisle, looking at him. The old man was somewhat out of context here in the city. He looked like he had just come from the farm. The old man was looking at him warmly. The creases of his face gave him a rumpled, well-lived-in expression.

"You don't look so good, boy," the old man said with a smile.

Stanley explained the sorry state of his affairs. The old man nodded.

"Yeah, that's a hard roll," he said. "But the truth is, sometimes in this life you get chicken and sometimes you get feathers," and he chuckled good-naturedly. "None of us can avoid it. That's just the way things are. Sometimes chicken, other times feathers."

Stanley found himself chuckling a bit also. It was good to share his thoughts with someone, and he liked the old man's chicken image. He answered with one of his own. "That's like, when life gives you lemons, make lemonade."

The old man nodded. "Which is the same as, 'a road without obstacles don't lead nowhere.'"

Stanley quickly replied: "Which is the same as, 'sometimes you get the dog, other times the dog gets you.'" And they both laughed.

The next stop was the old man's and he waved cheerily and got off. "Remember about the chicken, son," he called as he stepped off. Stanley sat and thought about this little encounter a long time. It was strange, he thought, that a few clichés should make so much difference in his mood. But there it was. A few words really did change his outlook.

This is the power of a word. This is the undiscovered power of an affirmation. A word has tremendous power to guide us. The mind tends to wander about here and there. The mind is often like a leaf caught in a storm. By utilizing words constructively, by narrowing our focus, we are able to accomplish things we never thought we could—including changing our mood.

Certain affirmations are common because they are true! Never forget this. They are true because they have withstood the test of time and brought greater clarity to people's lives.

It's a good practice to make or carry a small pad of paper or notebook that you exclusively devote to recording short, concise statements of truth. Keep your eyes and ears open for revelations of truth. Each time you hear and identity one, turn it into a statement and write it into your notebook. Often you will find these revelations in unlikely places. Don't worry if they don't resonate with your friends. Each person's book is unique. Just jot them down and review them several times a week—or, just when you need to. Choose one phrase that seems most meaningful and bring it to mind throughout the day. Everyone has key phrases—but remember these tend to change a bit week to week. Insights and understandings that resonate deeply are key tools in our spiritual practice. Find your personal resonators and begin to use them.

---

PART II

*Feel It*

# Making It Count

Does what you do count? Do your activities have any meaning, in the larger nature of things? Do your hopes and aspirations, your accomplishments, triumphs, and failures matter? You walk through your days and so many things happen. Some of them seem oddly coincidental and somehow interrelated. Others so random, they almost make your teeth hurt.

Knocking back and forth between the random and the planned, how should you try to see the unfolding of your life? This type of question arises in your heart at many odd moments. Of course, the question of meaning is expected to arise after defeat or crisis or tragedy, for your spirits are usually low then anyway. During challenging times, you are depleted, so you may have a tendency to view everything around you as depleted, random, and negative. Strangely, however, the question of meaning arises in the odd, benign moment, too.

Perhaps you wonder about it as you read the Sunday paper, or drive to work, or are out shopping for groceries. What are your actions worth and how is what you are doing connected to the larger picture?

Mary was an overachiever. She worked hard and had met many of her occupational goals but was still oddly dissatisfied. Though she was on the fast track of becoming a partner in her law firm and was clearly respected by the people she worked with during the day, doubts still continued to nag at her.

For a while Mary began doing meditation. Though she had always prided herself on being disciplined, she found this practice very difficult. She fell asleep almost every time she sat to meditate. A pragmatic woman, she began to meditate in her bed as she lay down to sleep. But then the meditation practice, which she had started as something meant to make her feel better and help move her toward meaning, started to feel like a burden also. As she thought about it, she started feeling guilty and nervous about this. What was the point of it? If it was to bring peace, it wasn't working, so perhaps she was not doing it right. This question began to nag at her and it led to other questions. She became more and more agitated and finally made an appointment with her instructor.

When they were sitting together she explained her situation, then blurted out the first question that arose in her mind: "If I meditate when I'm lying down, does it count?" When she asked this she had a vision of herself as a child asking whether her work would get a gold star in the teacher's book. Her meditation teacher laughed.

"Mary," he said. "It all counts."

And so it is in our life. Everything counts. People tend to see their lives as disjointed; broken pieces of a whole. Each moment seems to either be devoted to the good or the bad, and the good moments, in order to be good, must be done in a certain manner and at a certain time. You may tend to see life as sometimes making sense and sometimes not, and torturing yourself about this. But the truth is, regardless of what the final, ultimate "truth" is, it all counts. You can recognize that everything you do touches someone. Like ripples of a pond, everything reaches out and affects everything else. So it all counts.

Everyone's life is a continuum (with admittedly profound, transforming moments that arise), each part pouring like a cup of water into the next. Whoever you are in that moment, why, that is just who you are.

It all counts. Each moment influences the next and helps to define your direction. Everything counts because everything is within the moment. The moment is the sum of yourself for just that instant. No more, no less. Each moment then becomes an opportunity, whether lying in your bed or sitting in a straight-backed position.

To practice and deepen this awareness, for the next few days take on the discipline of a verbal formula. For example, as you do the various mundane things we all do, just think, or softly articulate: "This counts." As you brush your teeth, look in the mirror and say: "This counts." It's a little bit silly, but that's okay. It's still a very powerful technique, for it will bring you back to taking stock of yourself in a deep and transformative way. You will see the preciousness of the moment.

Everything counts.

# Two Types of Love

There are a thousand levels of love. But they can be divided into two main types. Does our love warm only us, or does it serve many around us? Is our love ultimately of benefit to us alone, or to many? The warmth of love is so great that we are often confused by it. We experience it and believe: "Ah, this is enough. I am warmed, there is no further I can go with this." But love is an ocean that ultimately has no end and no bottom. It is a well not only from which we can draw infinitely but also into which, spiritually speaking, we are prompted again and again to go deeper—to use it to reach out, even in the most humble and simple of ways. In this way, love not only fulfills ourselves and others but also continues to expand.

An easy exercise at home: Ask yourself, "What makes love triumphant?" If you think about it for a little bit, you will notice that love arises in our hearts naturally, not through force or threat. Indeed, such an idea—that I can threaten or force you to feel love—is absurd! So, how does love arise in our hearts? It is through its ability to utterly transform the soul upon which it operates. For when love enters a person, immediately many past patterns are put away and many inner darknesses are suddenly made light. This is even one of the abiding metaphors of love—that it is light. For it illuminates everything around it. This can perhaps be illustrated by a story.

Once there was a man who found himself lost in the forest. He wandered for many days and began to despair.

Suddenly in the gloom, he saw a light and rushed toward it. It was another person. "I am saved!" he shouted. "You can lead me out of here!"

"Get away," said the fellow. "I'm getting out and you'll slow me down." And he ran off.

The man lost in the forest was bereft and more heavyhearted than he had been. A little while later, another person came along with a lantern. Again the lost one ran up to him: "I am saved. Lead me out of here!"

The torchbearer laughed. "Well, perhaps you're saved," he said.

"What do you mean!" cried the lost one, despair in his voice. "How long have you been here?" he asked.

"Twenty years," replied the man with the light.

"Twenty years! Then we are doomed!" cried the lost man.

"Perhaps not," replied the other, putting his arm around his companion. "It is true I have been here a very long time. And it is also true that I am still lost. But the final truth is that I have charted many, many trails and I can tell you which ways not to follow. And we will be together."

And with these words they were both strengthened and comforted and so went on together.

One may not have all the truth, but we recognize that discovering our way out (regardless of what "out" means to you) rests with many others who help us and not just with our own strength or cleverness. We carry, in a manner of speaking, the light for each other. We recognize that we may not be altogether able to get out of the forest, but being with other people is an end in itself, and all will come clear in the end. When we are together, it does not seem like such a wilderness.

A good practice is to, every day, do a random act of kindness for someone. They don't need to know who has done this kindness for them. In fact, it is better if they don't know! Be imaginative. Put a quarter in a stranger's expired parking meter. Wash all the dishes in the sink, even if they're not all yours. Leave a ripe piece of fruit on your colleague's desk.

Try to do this for the sake of love. As you do it, repeat to yourself words to the effect: "I do this for the sake of love in the world. That others may benefit. That others may be enhanced by this act." Ultimately, we are all lost in the forest. We can only get out by using each other's light.

═══════════════════════════

# Thank Goodness!

Sometimes it can be difficult to identify life's overflowing opportunities and good fortune; but be assured they are present. Frequently, as we live our lives day by day, struggling can overshadow us. It's true, life's challenges can be overwhelming. And the demands and responsibilities quite often can feel insurmountable, or, at the least, extremely draining. Still, in every situation there always are circumstances for which to be grateful.

Lili, a thirty-six-year-old social worker, spends her days working with elder adults who are spending the last years of their lives in public facilities operated by strangers. A ninety-three-year-old resident, a delicate woman named Bell, had recently moved to the downtown facility. Bell is confined to a wheelchair.

On a winter day, with sunlight streaming through large bay windows, Bell, sweet as could be, was hunched over in a wheelchair that supports her spine, the strength of which osteoporosis stole years ago. Her physical paralysis was worse than in days past: her neck was cocked, her arms contorted, her eyes smoked by cataracts. She couldn't possibly be comfortable, but somehow Bell's posture seemed natural.

Walking briskly down the hall, Lili came to a complete stop just a few feet from Bell. She noticed Bell's chair was positioned by the door, waiting, as she did every day, for her visitors' to arrive—relatives and friends who had stopped calling long ago.

Lili was overcome with her own sadness. Nonetheless, she took a deep breath and mustered up the will to be upbeat, presumably for the sake of her client. "Hi ya, Bell," she said, as she reached around to adjust Bell's neck, relieving the strained muscles. "How are you today, my friend? Everything okay?"

"Oh yes, child," the elder whispered, "I am ever so blessed."

It's easy to be grateful when life circumstances are going well. But gratitude, as you know, can be difficult to identify when life seems more complicated, such as when you're stressed or nervous, frightened or overwhelmed.

The truth, however, is that there is always one thing—or, with a little thought, many things—for which you can be grateful. And when you're grateful, or at least aware of how fortunate you are, life just is a bit better. It's that simple.

Writing thank-you notes—whether to yourself, to the universe, or to another individual, will help you identify, acknowledge, and remember life's ever-present generosity. Although it's simple, it is guaranteed to make you more aware of the overflowing opportunity and good fortune that are yours everyday—regardless of whether your day was a bust or a celebration. Here's how it goes:

❖ Every day (or at least on many days), either first thing in the morning or at day's end, compose a thank-you note to whomever you like. In the note, either write down or speak aloud at least three things (and more if you want!) for which you are grateful that day.

❖ You can list general topics, such as health and friends, and you can list specific items, such as finding a five-dollar bill in the dryer after doing your laundry. Be aware that regardless of what you choose to include, these simple acknowledgments are of life's gifts to you.

Remember, a day is never all good or all bad. Simply and regularly acknowledging this fact brings the truth closer to your heart. You can keep these gratitude notes to yourself. Or, if you want, you can share them with people to whom you feel grateful. Either way, make the time today to write down or speak aloud things you're grateful for. You'll feel better and more alive—absolutely.

Today, I'm thankful for . . .

# Beyond Self-Imposed Limitations

Everyone has a way in which they would like to be seen by others, but even more important is how you see yourself. This is a well-known but easily forgotten truth. How you see yourself is who you live with day in and day out. The adjuration "Love your neighbor like yourself" really only has merit if you love yourself. That is, if you hate yourself, then loving your neighbor like that is not a great deal for them. If you start with the solid foundation of love for yourself (not conceit), and honest credulity that you are a creation of the infinite spirit, created in the image of the divine, then everything else will follow from that.

For example, fear is an emotion and response that every person, regardless of their self-image, experiences. Some people walk around with fear as a chronic condition, allowing it to unnecessarily define them. The fact is, everything feels fear, at least everything conscious. A chipmunk, for instance, feels fear when the fox is close. People, however, are able to fear so many more things—we have the skill to imagine things, and be afraid of what we imagine.

We are able to be afraid of things that haven't even begun to happen and are far away on the horizon, perceived only as possibilities! We can keep ourselves up at night about what is going to happen twenty years in the future. We can drive ourselves to a breakdown worrying about the future fact of the sun going nova.

When you try and reach beyond your fears or your sense of guaranteed safety, you will reap the most rewarding, enjoyable experience. It will open doors that you never knew existed.

Roger and his youngest daughter, Becca, for example, reached beyond their perceived fears when they went on a weekend kayaking excursion to the Russian River. The area is rich in bays and secluded bayous, and the river runs down into the sea. As they prepared to pitch their small kayak out into the river, Roger could see the ocean beating up the shore downstream. The froth from the waves hung a haze on the horizon, creating rainbows and sparkles that were beautiful, but the large waves also looked ominous. It was a chilly day and the water was kicking up a little. As his ten-year-old daughter disappeared into her life jacket, she looked out over the bay toward the pounding surf of the ocean.

"This really isn't such a good idea," she opined.

"No, you'll love it," her father said. "We're not going close to the ocean."

"No, I don't think so," she replied gravely. She looked anxious.

Roger said nothing. He tucked her into the back of the boat, handed her a paddle, and they pushed off. The water was very bouncy and, at first, Becca made disgruntled noises behind her dad. They pushed a little deeper into the bay. Suddenly the wind lightened and they floated with the water, moving gently up and down like a cork. The gulls floated above them and the water was the color of jade.

They stayed bobbing there for several minutes.

"Dad?" she said.

"Yeah?"

"It's really great. I'm glad you said to come out."

Life is always providing pause, providing reasons to fear. In the very youngest to the oldest, fears arise. Fear is a part of the gift of consciousness. But it's not the end of the story. Life always allows the possibility of pushing through your own self-imposed limitations. Even when you do push through your constraining ideas, it's difficult to admit that what you thought would be unpleasant is really quite transformative. Reaching beyond your limited ideas of what is "safe" is a daily opportunity.

Every day you are given the opportunity to push your limits in small and great ways. Try to let this be a daily exercise. Push yourself a tiny bit on one specific thing that you do. For example: Talk to a person you might otherwise avoid; or send in your poetry to be published; or speak out your opinion at a meeting. It's a small idea, but pushing beyond your small fears will have lasting effects.

# Generosity Is True North

You live your whole life giving and receiving. Certainly some types of giving (and receiving) seem higher and more profound to you than others. How do you share? Ultimately, what is the most important type of sharing or generosity?

Trying to cross the street, Doug was almost run down twice. It seemed that the people didn't only not slow down but also actually seemed to speed up to keep him from getting across the road. Several people signed obscenities at him. What was the world coming to, he thought. It sometimes seemed no one had any desire to give a little bit.

Later that day, Doug tried to reach out to his friends for support. He was feeling lonely and frustrated, but it seemed that everyone he called to make a time to get together with was busy and slightly distracted. None of them had time for him. He felt bad. He felt alone and, most painful, he felt lonely.

Doug craved interaction and rapport with another. Human connections commonly are equated with generosity, a giving of one's time. Why this is so is not immediately clear. Surely your heart wishes to be more generous—at least often, if not all the time. But why is this? Generosity is a quality that sustains and defines the entire universe. The very essence of your spirit—beneath your defenses and personal agendas—is generosity and the desire to share all good things.

Since this is the essence of the universe, we, who are created from that essence, continually yearn to emulate and embody this behavior. Generosity—giving from the heart—is true north, so to speak, and people are always seeking to point themselves in that direction.

Ultimately, you're most happy when you are generous and most troubled in spirit when you diverge from this direction. Generosity is a pathway toward intimacy and connection because the universe is generous and it is through this way of being that connection (of every type) thrives.

By evening, Doug had decided to go to the community dance hall, even though he felt even more lonely and withdrawn than he had earlier. If he didn't go, there was almost literally nothing else to do but stay home and watch the tube. He had not been out dancing since his teens, and the idea was a little horrifying. But there is nothing like pain to motivate action.

He found, surprisingly, the dance uplifted his spirits. During a break, an older gentleman stood in the circle of the crowd and held up a loaf of homemade bread. He asked everyone to touch the loaf of bread, or to touch someone who was touching the loaf, so that the whole group of dancers was united.

"Everything we own, we owe to somebody else," he said. "The clothes we wear, someone else made them. The car we drive, someone else mined the ore and refined the gas. Everything we have is because of someone else. Wherever or whatever God is, whether you call it heaven or enlightenment—one thing is sure, we can't get there solely by ourselves. We need each other."

For Doug, this became a core insight. He found himself looking at people a little differently. He found himself repeating this teaching to friends and colleagues. He found himself beginning to live a little differently. He saw his fellow beings more as partners than as just neutral entities whom he happened to interact with on a daily basis. People could be partners in the play of life, and seeing this lightened him. He realized he didn't have to do all the work himself. He realized that everyone was connected.

There are many ways to touch our own core of generosity. One exercise is to keep a small bowl of money next to the door. Whenever you leave the house, take a handful of change and promise yourself that for the sake of generosity you will distribute this particular money to people down on their luck, living on the street. And, each time you give away the money, make a promise to look at the person you are giving it to.

Such small gestures are what make up the meaning in our lives. They are how the world is changed.

---

# The "Who" of You

Beneath all of your materialistic acquisitions and psychological defenses, do you have a clear definition of *who* you are? Be aware: *who* you are is quite different from *what* you are. *Who* you are is based on your deep essential core; *what* you are is derived from a lifetime of expectations and responsibilities.

You were born with your *who;* you acquired your *what. Who* has a foundation of purity; *what* is based on personal need or advancement. Though the difference between the two may seem slight, the motivation of each is nothing like the other. Your *who,* for example, is committed, while your *what* is driven. Your *who* is grateful, while your *what* is appreciative. Concern comes from your *who;* worry comes from your *what.*

If you're older than the age of four or five, living a life based purely on *who* you are may seem impossible. As a conscientious, stable adult, your life most likely is directed—or at least heavily influenced—by assumptions, beliefs, hopes, and future dreams. Some of these expectations are your own and some come from the people you love, from those you are responsible for, and from society at large. How, for instance, do you live a life based solely on your *who* when you have a partner to support, a profession to manage, friends and family to take care of, bills to pay, health to deal with, and on and on and on.

Although living your *who* isn't easy, it most certainly is possible. In fact, your *who* is your most natural state of being. You organically experience your *who* when you make a choice based on what your heart feels as opposed to the pure logic of what your mind believes (or fears). Life exponentially heightens when your *who* directs and receives first billing in the grand movie of your life.

Jamie, a fun-loving, vivacious university coed, had the same boyfriend at twenty-one years old as she did when she was sixteen. Jamie never questioned whether her boyfriend was right for her, as he was the type of man she (and her family) had always expected she would marry. He was like a brother, lover, and friend all rolled into one. They would be together forever, she thought.

At the pool one day, Jamie met a man who didn't necessarily meet her "expectations" but who most certainly touched her heart. He was handsome, smart, funny, and sincere. At first they were "just friends," learning of the other's life, sharing strolls along the shoreline, laughing at personal jokes, and reveling in their intimate experiences together. Soon, Jamie began to wonder how she could continue to resist the *who* of her new friend. Although her longtime boyfriend had all of the *what* elements she desired, his *who* elements were obviously lacking.

"*Who* am I?" Jamie asked herself. "*Who* are these men? What will make me happier: a focused, successful, driven husband, or a sincere, intelligent life partner? Both were good men, but her new friend was the best long-term choice for her life and, ultimately, for her heart.

Certainly it can be difficult to distinguish between *who* you are and *what* you expect. In fact, it may often feel as if the *who* and the *what* of you are one and the same. Be aware: they are not. To know this with certainty, the *who* of you must learn to pull rank in all circumstances.

It isn't a mystery. You ultimately know who you are. Begin by recognizing and acting on small declarations of your *who*. When you must make a choice or take a stand, ask yourself to differentiate between your *who* and your *what*. As you begin to discern the unique qualities of each, you'll learn how your *who* can take precedence in significant situations. Eventually—from phone calls to taxes to marriage—you'll crave that your *who* dictate all decisions. The greatest sin of being alive is to want to be something you are not. Forget the *what*. Learn to look within yourself and accept the *who* of you.

# The Eyes of the Heart

Few situations or objects are exactly as they seem. They often are much more than just their appearance. Just as there are certain places (like the Grand Canyon) that by their presence alone have power to open our spirits, so there are objects that by their pure nature illumine us.

Maddy had a six-year-old daughter who made her a ceramic bowl at school. It was a class project and every child had to make their parent some ceramic gift. The bowl her daughter, Hale, made for her was lopsided, and the green and yellow color scheme was streaked and muddied. The bowl did not exactly balance; it tended to rock back and forth with the merest touch. Yet when Maddy received it she realized that it was the most beautiful ceramic bowl that had ever been made. It was far and away more precious than the bowls she had seen in museums, or the expensive crockery or glassware that filled her house. This bowl was absolutely and without question the most beautiful bowl ever made. She held it up and oohed and aahed over it. Her daughter beamed with pleasure.

"Do you really like it, Mommy?" she asked.

"It is the most beautiful bowl ever made," she repeated to her daughter.

Her daughter clapped her hands with pleasure at being able to create and to give to her mother the most beautiful bowl in the world, and then she bounced off to play with her toys.

Maddy sat with the bowl in her lap. Her realization was not something subjective, it was actually so. She hugged her daughter and thanked her again that evening when they used the bowl to serve broccoli (though some of the juice ran out from the bottom). When Maddy mentioned the ceramic bowl to her friend Sara the next day, Sara was silent a moment. "You know our children are in the same class, and though I don't want to take anything away from your daughter, my son also made a bowl that I realized last night was the most beautiful bowl ever made. We used it as a serving dish for dinner. So, though I am willing to say that your daughter's is the second most beautiful, I am afraid I cannot go along with you in saying it is the most beautiful. That honor, you see, already belongs to my child's creation."

They went on in this vein for a while, without rancor, trying to convince the other of what they said. As their days progressed, they ran into other friends whose children had made various types of objects, pitchers and glasses, bowls and tie racks, garlic holders and pipe cleaner figures. Each one, the parent realized, was the very best and most perfect one ever made.

The truth was each of them was correct. You might think this is impossible, but it is not so. It's one of the miracles of day-to-day life that we are blessed to witness. There can be a thousand objects, made by a thousand different pairs of hands, yet each one is the best one made—ever. As long as we see things with the eyes of flesh, then a thing is merely a thing to be weighed in competition. But when we see with the eyes of the heart, then we see a thing in an entirely new way.

The eyes of the heart are how you can see each person, each tree, each moment. Each person is the very crown of creation. Perfect in their mold, beautiful in their guise. How can this be so? You can see each person with the eyes of the heart instead of with eyes of flesh. It's the same logic that makes people act their highest when conditions are at the lowest.

Take a little time and make something for a friend or a loved one. It doesn't need to be profound; it doesn't even have to balance. It can be as simple as a napkin drawing, or a small tree you planted in a personally painted pot. The recipient of your gift doesn't need to treasure it. For the love that imbues it will be enough. Over time, viewing your life and people you love through the eyes of the heart will transform you.

---

# Emotionally Numb

There is no aspect of your emotional being that can or will spontaneously develop on its own. Even your natural tendencies, such as compassion and love, must be nurtured. Only with practice will your emotions unfold to their full flower. Everything must be practiced, or you risk atrophy.

Many people describe emotional atrophy as "feeling numb." There is no other way to say it. Worse, they feel that there is no real way to change or improve feeling numb. Ultimately the only thing standing in your way is failure to continually practice moving toward your true potential. You must have an active desire to reach your true being. Whatever you allow yourself to feel, that is who you will become.

Jan, for example, couldn't understand why she always felt emotionally numb, especially at the most inappropriate times. Recently, Jan had heard about the suffering of a friend and sympathized, but in the privacy of her home she acknowledged that she was strangely unmoved. Indeed, she found the friend's sadness and needs and tears oddly annoying. She read in the paper about the pain in the world and the tragedies that seemed to infest every corner of life, and she was left with a certain coldness.

"Not much gets through that armor of yours," her last boyfriend had said to her. "You say all the right things and make the right replies, but I don't really think you *feel* much of anything."

"Well I don't go around blubbering for the whole world like you," she snapped.

"There's a difference between blubbering, as you call it, and being genuinely touched by the conditions of others," he said. "It's not that you don't feel, it's just you don't let it get very deep inside before you squelch it. Ultimately, that's what makes a person unhappy. It just leaves a person frozen and miserable."

Alone in her apartment, alone with herself and her thoughts, Jan acknowledged that much of what he had said was true. There were good reasons for her being the way she was. She had learned early to armor herself. But still, the consistent echoing of numbness was a feeling she wanted to change.

To unblock the heart so that it can feel more deeply and truly is a difficult task. The following four steps will lead you to opening your emotional bouquet:

1. First, recognize and make the decision that ultimately an armored life is not what you really want. Nor is it the true destiny of any human being. Misery is not the fate of humanity. Your history does not have to be your destiny.

2. The second is to practice simple visualizations of compassion. Imagine people or creatures in the condition of travail. For example, picture in your mind's eye a child who has been hurt, or is lost from its parents, unable to find them. Imagine their fear and pain and their deep longing for succor. This step can be difficult, as these types of visualizations are difficult because they can play on your own fears of pain, loss, and abandonment. Be strong and persevere in your practice. Eliciting and deepening the quality of mercy, love, and compassion is one of the highest things you will ever do in your life.

3. The third step is to visualize real situations occurring in your community. For example, choose a person or two randomly from your day—perhaps someone you see on the bus or who delivers memos to your office. Try to imagine conditions of existential or physical difficulty they may be experiencing and try, through that visualization, to personally feel what they may be facing.

4. Last, think sweet thoughts of healing for these people and say them aloud, either to the person or just under your breath (so no one else can hear). Linger with these thoughts and with your visualizations.

Begin using this four-step process to lighten the load of feeling emotionally numb. Seeing people less and less as *other* and as more connected with you personally will help you begin to open.

The opportunity of this work exists all around you, in the checkout line, for example, or in chance encounters in a movie theater. Developing mercy and compassion is the antidote to numbness.

# Large Fear, Small Fear

It is a cliché, but a very true one, that life is uncertain. No one can know what his or her future is. This fact can be either liberation for you or a great weight. It is natural and right for you to try to control your environment in such a way that you minimize problems or dangers. But it is also imperative that you recognize that nothing ever fully protects you. Life itself is meant to be somewhat unsafe—that's the very nature of existence.

No one can live in a bubble, and even if we could, it would be a ferociously boring sort of existence. Part of the charm of life is not only its great uncertainty but also its pain. For the nature of pain is often to force us to grow to a higher understanding of joy and wisdom (painful as the process itself often is).

Susan decided it was time to move from her neighborhood. It had changed over the last few years and was not as safe as it once was. There were more and more muggings. There had even been a rash of daytime burglaries over the last few months. Though she herself had never had any problems, she knew people who had been hassled and her next-door neighbor had been robbed. Yes, it was time to move, she thought.

Susan was well-liked by everyone, and people were sad to see her go. She had been active in the neighborhood, working with the children in tutorial reading programs, active in neighborhood cleanups, and more. All the neighbors threw her a big party and warned her to be careful in New York, which was where she was moving. She had found and purchased a lovely little flat in Brooklyn on a tree-lined, almost crime-free street. Unfortunately, the renovation was not complete when she arrived so she rented a flat in lower Manhattan. Two days after moving into the rental, the World Trade Center was destroyed and her apartment was ripped apart by the debris. Fortunately, Susan was at work and escaped personal injury, but all of her belongings were destroyed.

There is a certain irony in life that is inescapable. Events shape you. People travel to a certain place to be safe, and it is exactly there that disaster falls. People yearn for safety, but in the final analysis safety is impossible to fully achieve. There is something in the human mind that recognizes this truth but finds it very difficult to accept.

One thing that is clear is how much the emotion of fear is part of a larger attitude. You can spend a lot of time thinking about all the different kinds and parts of fear that arise and dominate your life. It is disquieting how many fears there are! Fear of traveling. Fear of strangers. Even fear of opening mail. A fear of crowded places, high-rises, government offices, people from other countries—the list goes on. When we feel a fear, it is obviously something that has to be acknowledged. Fear is far too strong to pretend it doesn't exist. Sometimes, such as in Susan's case, fear is well founded. But many fears are like the genie of Aladdin's lamp: they are only smoke. They may look very imposing, very solid, but, finally, they are still only smoke.

Here is a recommended game to incorporate into your daily life. Take a piece of paper and write down some of the fears that are currently holding you back from what you could be or the way you would like to be. Enumerate them, big and small. Look at them and accept that they are your fears.

Resolve to take them with you as you go forward but not to let them dominate you. Then burn the piece of paper. After a day or two, write them out again. See if they are the same fears and notice how they begin to change. Over time, your awareness of your fears and your conscious burning of them, or letting them go, will lessen their grip on your movement through life. Remember, you are the bus driver. Let your fears be passengers, not conductors of your life.

---

# Universal Download

The greatest mystery is you. This is an insight so fundamental that it should be kept printed on a little card that is placed in plain sight, always. Each person is a hero. Each person is a work of art.

The single greatest difficulty in realizing this truth is learning to live with what you are given. For most folks, embracing life involves a great deal of uncertainty, pain, and adversity. But there is a way in which even these things—these states of being—must be seen as friends. This is the first part of learning to live with (and then love) what unfolds in your life. Half of everything learned in this life comes in the form of a difficult lesson. It is necessary to understand the lesson, incorporate it, and then hopefully move on from it. Always, however, part of every lesson involves reshaking the seltzer bottle of yourself and letting it gush out in a new way.

Dana, a young woman, left the university for a sabbatical to study yoga. After about six months studying with her instructors, she realized she was not really enjoying the process of learning yoga nearly as much as she had thought she would. She went to one of her instructors and told him about her relative "dis-ease." Her teacher nodded, his face grave. He bent over a piece of paper and wrote on it. Then he folded it and handed it to her. On the front of it he had written: "Each moment is a special moment." On the inside, it read: "A Thelma and Louise moment."

It took her a moment to figure out what he meant. Then she smiled. Then she laughed. He was telling her that every moment was, in a manner of speaking, a leap of faith, and this leap was essentially into the void of not knowing. Every moment is an exercise: learning to live with what you are given, with whatever you have done, and learning to be as completely committed to it as possible. Each activity requires a uniquely committed approach. Dana realized that she was trying to do her yoga studies in the same way she did her academic sociology studies, and it just didn't really work that way. Later, discussing it with her friends in the class, they reiterated what the instructor had written. "Don't try to learn this stuff as a profession; don't take it like a vitamin because it's 'good' for you; rather learn yoga as an art."

Dana's friend Mary chimed in: "It's the same difference between a profession and a celebration. In a job, the result is the thing. But a party, a celebration, the act itself is why it's important."

Yoga was a way for Dana to become more alive. She realized that she enjoyed it most when she didn't actually *think* about it but just did it. The universe has no way to manifest its will and desire except through creation, of which you are a shining example. The universe is constantly trying to download through you. The Infinite is trying to concretize itself through life, which means you. Part of your task is just to let it have expression, not only through the good but also in the realizing of the difficult.

In order to explore this understanding, it can be helpful (and fun) to put together a "universe expanding kit." This kit consists of items that inspire you. Examples of objects include pens, colors, pieces of fabric, handmade papers, sequins, inspiring quotes, photographs, note cards, etc. These are things by which you recognize and realize the greatest mystery (your life), and experience the universe downloading through you. Letting the universe do this helps to create an infinite, splendid succession of universally expansive moments. Each one, whatever it is, helps you realize that this moment you are given is the only "this moment" you are ever going to be given. So it is best to take full advantage of it. Each moment is a gate for the universe to speak through. However you speak and whatever you do, the Infinite is manifesting itself through you.

―――――――――――――――――――――

# A Mighty Bit of Faith

Faith. So powerful is this word, people seem unable to get away from it, especially when they begin talking about things that are really important. Certainly faith means different things to different people. Regardless of how you specifically define it, though, it is a word and a sentiment that moves you to great, even heroic action. For faith, a person often will sacrifice their life, their ambition, their future.

Recognizing the power of faith in our lives and its ability to move and (more important) to transform us is a vital step in a successful spiritual practice. A person is willing to sacrifice so much in the name of faith because they perceive that they are likely to receive so much more from their actions.

Sam was teaching in southern California at a youth offender institution. His job was to bring meditation and self-calming techniques to the young inmates. It was arduous and frustrating, because they were constantly making jokes and belittling what he did, but at the same time it was thrillingly rewarding work. When one of them opened up, even a little, Sam felt like he was witness to a miracle. During one group discussion, a young inmate spoke of his life, which had been one of abandonment and stark cruelty.

Left to fend completely on his own at a very young age, he had gone into the gang world and was only a step away from the perpetual living nightmare that career criminals often fall into. As he talked, describing his life, the other boys nodded their heads. Though he spoke dispassionately, his words were deeply affecting. Many of the others had experienced what he described. Certainly all had experienced hard knocks and bad choices.

"I'm going to tell a story," he said. Everyone fell silent. He was older than the other boys and was known as a powder keg, always just one step away from violence.

"Once there was a kid whose dad told him to pull up a stump that was in the middle of a field," he began. "This kid struggled and pulled and pushed and whacked at that stump for all he was worth. He tried as hard as he could, using a pick, using a shovel, using a lever. Finally he collapsed next to the stump, almost crying.

The father tramped off in disgust. "You better finish that before I get back," he yelled at the kid.

Time passed and an old man, a neighbor, came by and sat on a stone and watched the kid continue to struggle. The boy knew his father was serious and that he damn well better move that stump.

"You about finished?" the old man asked the boy.

"I've used everything," the boy gasped. "The shovel, a pick. I just can't get that stump out."

"There's one thing you haven't used," the neighbor said.

"What's that?"

"Me," he replied.

All the boys remained silent. It was a story that touched their hearts—not least because by telling it, the older boy was saying that one couldn't give up, that there was a reason to have faith—even if we didn't see it right away; even if the going got really hard. He was saying that even if one sort of support fails, it doesn't mean that there is no support. It means only that we must reach out, again and again if necessary.

Faith is a type of confidence; it is confidence in action, even if the action requires staying still. True faith is attempting to utilize everything we have at our disposal to bring about the desired result.

Make a list of things you have faith in. How can these faiths move you to a place higher than you are now? Learn to recognize and utilize your innate faith and develop deeper faith of your own. By keeping faith in the forefront of your heart, you will move more freely and be more open to the world around you.

# The Joy of Connection

There are two main yearnings in a person's heart. One is for joy and the other is for understanding. But really, these are two halves of the same thing. Understanding *is* joy, and joy, when it is true, is *always* about connection and understanding. Of all the connections possible, the most profound is when a human face is able to look upon another and see the truth of that person's humanity shining out.

Every person represents a miracle, and when we can see this it influences the very essence of how we treat each other, which, ultimately, is most important. Adam learned this lesson when he came face-to-face with the meter maid—a person he had normally thought of as his "enemy."

One day, Adam was sitting in his office on the thirty-fourth floor of a downtown high-rise when he realized that he had only two minutes left on his meter. He ran as fast as he could to get there. As he turned the corner, panting, running toward his car, he saw the fearsome bright green ticket being placed on his window. The meter maid who was ticketing him was about fifty, heavyset, with bright bleached hair. She moved slowly. She looked tired.

When Adam first saw her, he felt an angry shout begin to rise to his lips. But he pulled it back and instead strolled over to her as she started to get back into the little electric car.

"I guess I didn't quite make it," he said.

"Nope," she replied, noncommittally, not meeting his eyes. Adam realized in that very moment that what she was doing was a thankless job and that she probably received a lot of abuse for it through the day. So, instead of getting angry, he laughed. Startled, she looked at him with a question on her face.

"I bet a lot of people go off on you during a day," he repeated his thought out loud, with a smile in his voice.

"You're not kidding," she said, and the corners of her mouth turned a little.

"Life is about more than a ticket," he said. "No reason to get so hot about it. You're just doing your job."

"Well thanks," she said. "You'd think people would realize that, but they just don't. I could tell you stories," and she sighed.

"Tell me one," he suggested. And so she did. For the next fifteen minutes or so she told him stories. She told him about the circus clown who tried to sic a leopard on her. She told him about folks who called her a communist, a fascist, a tool of the government, and worse names too awful to repeat. As she told her story, her mood lightened and by the end of it they were both laughing at the absurd lengths people will go to for a few bucks.

"You know, they've been checking our ticket books lately," she said, kind of shyly, "and since I've already written the ticket, I can't really . . ."

"No, don't even think about it," said Adam . "It's all right. Like I said, you've got a job to do. No problem."

And with that, her face positively lit up. They waved good-bye to each other.

A week later, Adam realized again that he was late and again—thirty-four floors later—ran for his car. This time, as he rounded the corner, he saw a note on his window. It read: "I put a quarter in the meter for you. Take care now, and beware of the meter maids—signed Martha, the meter maid." It was his friend.

From that time forward, whenever he saw her, he waved. Sometimes he would stop his car and she her electric golf cart and they would exchange stories and laughs of the week. There was no reason really, it was just enjoyable to take a break and examine the human condition—as they both experienced it. Sometimes he would get a ticket (though he noticed never from Martha), but tickets didn't really bother him like they used to. When all was said and done, it was just a ticket.

The human need for connection is greater than anything else in life. One of the most important aspects of connection is being allowed to tell your story to another person. It's all about joy and understanding. When you are allowed to tell your story, the angels themselves stop in their busy round of duties on high and patiently listen.

---

# Finding True Home

Some people go through their whole life wondering where they belong. They feel uneasy and sad and afraid that, in reality, they don't really belong anywhere. They try many strategies of belonging. Businesses, to a great extent, rely on our deep inner yearning to belong. This often feeds our desire to buy something because buying is such a wonderful distraction.

Like the need for food or water, people cannot do without connectedness, without the feeling of belonging. Kari had always been a strongly driven career person. She had graduated from law school at a very young age, went immediately into business, and soon rose to a high position in her firm. One of her colleagues, envious about her rapid rise, asked her: "How do you do it? What is your secret?"

Pleased that he had asked, and proud of her accomplishments, she replied: "I keep my eyes on what is important and I don't let anything stand in my way." Kari traveled a great deal. Her apartment in New York City was very different from the home she had grown up in. In fact, it could not have been more different. Her apartment was painted in neutral pastels and the kitchen possessed a large refrigerator that held only the clichéd bottle of ketchup. Her furniture was expensive but spare, and her apartment had very few personal items. She was rarely home and always busy.

It was a major shock to Kari's schedule when her father died. Her sisters met her at the airport and they drove to the hospital. There they watched while the nurse turned off the respirator. She watched as her father drew his last breath. That night she and her sisters went back to their parents' home. "It's been a long time since I was here," she thought as she wandered from room to room. The house smelled of something familiar. She decided it smelled of memories. "This is my home," she thought and ran her hand over books that she remembered reading as a child. She sat down on the stairs and wept. What was a home, finally, she wondered. She realized that a home was not a room with furniture. It was not the four walls, nor the bric-a-brac. It was not necessarily even a person's birthplace. Home was a place where, when all was said and done, you belonged. Home was a place where a person experienced the state of belonging, belonging without question. A place where you realized, absolutely, you were not alone.

Where do you belong? Where is your home? If, in pondering this question, no satisfying answer arises, then it is time to take action. Without a sense of belonging, life becomes terribly frustrating. To help you clarify what makes you feel at home—like you belong—you can make a list of the things that remind you of where you come from and who you are. For example, your list may include the smell of lilacs that once grew in your mother's garden, taking a stroll along a riverside, or an old friend with whom you've lost touch. Think about your list in small, two- or three-minute chunks at first, jotting down whatever you come up with. Do this seven or eight times over the course of a day. Revise the list during the next couple of weeks.

At the end of the period, sit down with the list and make a sub-list of things that seem to appear repeatedly. You may be surprised by what you come up with. You will find yourself returning again and again to those experiences and things that remind you of where you belong and who you are. Choose one of the items on your list and commit to bringing it into your current life. You don't have to change your life to experience a sense of belonging, you just need to do those activities that create the feeling of what home means for you. So, pick some fresh lilacs to display in your kitchen, schedule a walk in nature, or call that old friend with whom you've lost touch. Keep your list handy and use it as a gateway to creating that sense of belonging that you crave.

---

# PART III

# Act It

# Look Them in the Eyes and Smile

Sometimes there is nothing sweeter than when someone looks you in the eyes and simply connects with you. No matter how rushed or irritated, gleeful or contemplative you are, when you see yourself reflected in the eyes of another, even just for a second, something inside of you is relieved. Whether you consciously identify it or not, in that fleeting but timeless exchange recognition and relief seep deep into your soul, allowing you to feel profoundly human and alive.

Regardless of the overwhelming health and emotional benefits that come from connecting with others, intimate eye-to-eye contact commonly is reserved for people who feel emotionally secure with one another: family members, friends, loved ones. Rarely, at least in the twenty-first century, is this exclusive arrangement questioned. Too often, this type of reserved intimacy is limiting, unconsciously creating feelings of disconnection, isolation, and loneliness.

Of course, in today's world, you have to be smart and aware of your surroundings, but rarely do you have to shut yourself completely off from everyone in order to feel safe. As you're walking down the street, for instance, you have the opportunity to communicate and connect—albeit briefly—with many people. A simple smile, a slight nod, a brief eye-to-eye connection: it's harmless and, for a moment, assures both individuals of their basic human core.

Pamela, a twenty-three-year-old business consultant who worked downtown, constantly passed hundreds of people on the street as she walked from a twenty-four-dollar-a-day parking garage to the fifty-six-floor building in which she spent her days. For the most part, she kept her head up and her eyes peeled straight ahead as she wound her way down crowded streets and subway terminals that were filled with others who had similar morning routines. Rarely did Pamela talk with or look directly at anyone—especially when she would reach into the bottom of her purse to find spare change to give to one of many street people holding out their jars.

One morning, Pamela read an article on the increased homeless population in her town. A longtime employee from the U.S. State Department strongly stated that people should not hand out money to street people. Instead, she recommended, "just look them in the eyes and smile. That one gesture is worth more than any money you could give to them."

So Pamela tried it the very next day. As she emerged from the parking garage, a homeless man asked her for spare change. She turned and smiled, saying, "Have a good day." The light ignited in the man's eyes as he fully felt the effects of the exchange.

"Lady," he said, "that smile is good enough for me. Bless you."

It can be challenging to connect with someone you don't know, especially a homeless person. The truth remains, however, that connection is the essence of being alive. It will awaken something inside you and inside them.

Twenty-eight-year-old Tesilya tried this simple exercise on her way to work one day. As she walked by her neighbor, she smiled. Instantaneously, the man began to recite poetry to her and her heart swelled.

It's just about that simple. Today, just once, randomly choose someone with whom to connect. As you pass them in the hall or on the street, look them in the eyes and smile. You'll notice, in that brief second, you'll escape your single-focused mind-set of accomplishment. In that passing moment, whatever you were doing or trying to do will simply cease to exist—you'll be fully, although briefly, connected with another.

If doing this with a complete stranger feels like too much of a stretch for you, begin with an acquaintance, someone in your office building, for instance, or someone who lives down the block from you. Choose a situation or a person in which you feel at least slightly comfortable but with whom you haven't before connected.

As your lips arch into a smile and your eyes meet with another's, something special ignites inside of you. It's the instantaneous bridge of sincere recognition and relief being built between you and your neighbor. It's simple as a gesture, but it's as profound as humanity.

# Doodle toward Divinity

If for just a few minutes a day you weren't thinking about anything—if you simply were being—your energy would increase, your outlook on life would gain positiveness, and the sense of order you crave would be more attainable. Yet, with crazy obligations and too few hours in the day, it often seems outrageous to believe you could devote effort and time to slow down enough to simply live only in the present moment without a thought of what you need to do, what you've already done, or what you wish you were doing.

It doesn't actually take much time or effort to practice mindfulness, a state of being where your body and mind relax and slow enough that you can honestly (but nonjudgmentally) feel what is occurring in your present moment. You needn't sit on a meditation cushion for hours a day or find a guru to lead you through complicated breathing exercises. In fact, you can actually be mindful (and reap the benefits of it) while you're engaged in activities that you do every day.

Walking, for example, is a mindfulness practice that you already do. In many spiritual traditions, people use walking to center themselves, using their steps to become aware of the sensations and thoughts streaming through their bodies and minds.

Mindfulness isn't about stopping all activity or changing your routines; it's about being aware. Mindfulness leads to awareness, which improves your health and increases your vitality.

Try it. See what you feel like when you walk mindfully. Start simply. The first step is choosing a destination, such as the car, and walking toward it with the awareness that you are walking. That's it. Just try to stay aware of the fact that you're walking five hundred yards to your car. You'll probably forget within ten seconds that you're walking. If you do, that's okay. Once you realize you're not thinking about walking, start thinking about it again.

Little by little you can add awareness to your mindful walking. Some further suggestions for mindful walking include:

* ❖ Concentrate on the inhalation and exhalation of your breath.

* ❖ Feel the weight of your body shift from your left foot to your right or from the heel to the ball of your foot.

Walking, along with other simple activities such as brushing your teeth, drawing on paper, eating a meal, answering the telephone, turning on your computer, opening the mail, are everyday opportunities to practice mindfulness.

Start with a ten-second goal, which means that you intend—for ten full seconds—to stay single-mindedly aware of the activity in which you are engaged.

Jack, a forty-two-year-old accomplished architect, chose to mindfully doodle his way to divinity. (Doodling is a mindfulness practice with roots that reach back long before the ballpoint pen.) Wishing to be more mindful, Jack decided to be aware for a minimum of ten seconds every time he found himself doodling. First, he simply tried to simultaneously doodle and be aware of the fact that he was doodling—a task he found difficult to accomplish. After a while, he added the awareness of holding his pencil, of noticing what position his hand was in, of feeling the texture of the pen cradled between his fingers. Eventually, Jack added the conscious awareness of the inhalation and exhalation of his breath while he doodled.

It was difficult at first, as Jack loved to lose himself in his drawing and doodling. Still, before long he found that his awareness not only made doodling fun but also began to provide insight, clarity, and a sense of stillness to boot. What used to be mindless ink and lead markings on paper soon led Jack to feeling less stressed and more refreshed throughout his day.

Ten seconds of mindfulness a day is the start of a fresh approach and perspective to your routines. You can't deny that you have ten seconds to spare. Try it. You'll find that mindful activity is more difficult to accomplish than you believe, but its effects are far grander than you imagine.

# As the Seasons Turn

Each turning of a season is an ephemeral passage of splendor: when the warmth of spring evaporates the wet chill of winter; when the brisk fall air dances against the heat of summer days. Nothing is quite as fresh as the smell of changing seasons; no colors compete with the brilliance of those that permeate distinct times of year.

The changing of the seasons not only offers dramatic aesthetic pleasures but also signals a perfect occasion—four times a year—for you to assess what you are doing, prepare for upcoming transformation, and embrace changes that are imminent.

Every quarter year, you have the opportunity to create a ritual around the upcoming season. See if any of the following seasonal celebrations appeal to you.

**Winter:** Take time during the winter season to assess your inner life. The days become shorter and shorter during this time of year, making it the perfect season to be indoors more often. Make a list of rejuvenating goals and priorities, which could include: nesting in your home, reading, renting movies, writing in your journal, and catching up on personal and house projects. On the eve of the winter solstice, which is the shortest day of the year and typically arrives sometime in the third week of December, cook a festive candlelit meal and write in your journal or verbally share with a loved one the goals you have for the coming new year.

**Spring:** As the days lengthen and the air begins to warm, be ready to burst outside in celebration. Springtime is the freshest time of year, perfect for planting the seeds of ideas and aspirations you've been storing all winter. Spring is the time of year when you can actively implement changes you imagined during the colder months. Spring allows you to follow through on the very items that previously were just good ideas. For example you might join an art class, begin hiking with a new club, or check out the local sailing team. You might want to spend more time enjoying the outdoor hobby of gardening while simultaneously pursuing your dream job of being an independent landscape artist. Springtime is a fresh, blossoming time of year; it's a delightful time to begin the active pursuit of dreams and inspirations you were thinking of all winter.

**Summer:** As the sun continues to extend its stay in the sky, the bright summer days make for long hours of warmth and sunshine. Look forward to celebrating the summer solstice, the absolute longest day of the year. On that evening, plan a walk to one of your favorite destinations, maybe one that overlooks the entire city skyline. The solstice is halfway through the year, so you might choose to spend the evening assessing how your goals, hopes, and dreams for the year are progressing. This ritual is a helpful time to reevaluate and redefine how you intend to spend the year's remaining six months.

**Fall:** The glory of fall arrives just in time to remind you that the high activity of the summer is beginning to fade and the restful, rejuvenating winter season is just around the corner. Fall is a time of harvesting. During fall, you reap the benefits of all your hard work and ideas from the year. It's a time of gratitude for all your success and struggle, for the opportunities and relationships you experienced during the year. As a ritual, you could choose to spend some time during Thanksgiving weekend at a city charity, donating your time and energy to sharing abundance and joy with others.

Whether it's the harvest moon rising above the horizon, the changing colors of the hilltops, or the bursting forth of flower gardens, the turning of each season is a perfect time to create seasonal celebrations for growth, opportunity, and goal setting.

If you have a partner or friend with whom you can participate, that's great. It can be fun to share your ideas and hopes with another. If you're more of a lone seeker, the process is just as engaging. Either way, be sure to calendar seasonal dates in your appointment book and honor keeping them as you would a professional commitment. You'll see, as the seasons turn, so will your motivation, intentions, and direction.

# A Date with Destiny

Though you may be pleased with your life, you may also occasionally sense that something is missing. Nothing is glaringly wrong; in fact, when you think about it, you're probably quite happy with how you're humming along day after day. Yet, in the very back of your mind, or the pit of your stomach, you know that things either aren't quite as they should be or that they could become just a bit better. They always can, right?

When you feel a little off kilter, when you have that irksome sense of "why?" or "how?" schedule a date to check in and mindfully converse with Destiny, that force within you that guides you toward your perfect truest self.

Mark, a thirty-four-year-old business coach, schedules a weekly appointment with Destiny. In fact, Destiny is one of his most consistent clients: they have tea together every Monday among the eclectic klatch at an upgraded, funky 1920s teahouse. At a quiet table tucked away in a corner, he sips green tea, inhales the fresh Asian-accented aroma, and exhales. "What is next?" he asks, and then pauses. Another breath. "What is next?" His hand, poised above a pad of paper, writes down whatever comes to mind; whatever his heart reveals; whatever thoughts pass through him. Sometimes, Mark gains such profound insight that he's surprised it didn't come from a two-hundred-dollar-an-hour business consultant. How is it possible, he wonders, that simply by focusing one's attention, creating the space to listen, and being openhearted without specific goals can result in such strong feedback? Other weeks, Mark isn't blown away by insights; he simply feels more grounded and present with a stronger sense of calm.

Whether your time is limited or you can afford to spend an entire day hanging out at the beach, your aim is the same: release all expectation of who you are and what you are supposed to be doing, and suspend any and all notions of your personally identified goals. Don't worry, as soon as your date with Destiny is over, you can reengage all sense of personally driven purpose—though you may find your direction is slightly (or dramatically!) altered.

Here's what you can do:

**First, steal or schedule quality moments.** If you are extremely limited in time, take advantage of the moments you're waiting in line, stuck in traffic, or on hold during a telephone call. Although brief, you'll be relieved at what concentrated doses of Destiny will bring. If you have the time, make an appointment with Destiny for an hour or more. Write the appointment down or key it into your calendar, and honor it as you would a date with a friend or a colleague.

**Ask gently, "What is next?"** Once you arrive at your date, settle down and take a few deep breaths. You can do this with your eyes opened or closed (if you're in traffic—keep your eyes open!). Ask gently, "What is next?" Pause and listen. Then, do it again: breathe in, exhale, and ask: "What is next?" Pause and listen.

It's okay if you don't receive insight right away. Just keep breathing, asking, and listening. If you're standing in line waiting for the next teller window to open, the answers you receive may be brief. On the other hand, if you've invited Destiny for coffee hour, you can expect to receive more than a brief explanation of your situation. In both cases, however, the hospitable nature of Destiny will always leave you with a deeper sense of clarity, connection, and, if you're fortunate, some guidance.

**Take notes.** Sometimes it's beneficial to jot down a few notes about what you're feeling, thinking, or sensing. Did a fresh insight about your son flash across your mind? Maybe a mental image went fleeing by of a colleague at the office or of a family member. On occasion, entire dialogues may unfold right inside your head and heart: step-by-step instructions pouring into your consciousness. Whatever unfolds, it's always beneficial to write it down, or make a note of it. Insights are slippery, you know; they, like your nighttime dreams, can slip away, even when you believe you'll remember them forever.

Not everyone has time to schedule a weekly date with Destiny. Yet, even stolen moments can generate a stronger sense of groundedness, peace, and clarity. If you're fortunate, a little bit of wisdom may slip in, too.

---

# Court the Unexpected

On any given day, you never know what you can expect. Miracles seemingly fall from the sky, tragedies sometimes arrive instantaneously, and fun occasions present themselves at the most unlikely of moments. When opportunities arise, it's best if you're prepared to make the absolute most of them.

Learning to follow through on your intuition is the best way to be prepared for every situation. That means not only listening closely to your inner voice but also fully heeding its call, regardless of how far-fetched the information may seem to be. You have to keep your sanity, of course. You don't want to mindlessly follow through on ideas; you want to make sound, clearheaded decisions. Yet, many thoughts float through your head and heart that are completely ignored. Most of them, in fact, don't even register on your Richter scale of significance.

According to one university study, most people have six thoughts a day that, if followed through on, could make them millionaires. Imagine, if that's true, how many thoughts a day you must have that would significantly increase your spiritual worth. If you followed through on half the generous, considerate, morally uplifting ideas that swiftly pass through your mind, you'd be spiritually affluent in no time.

Following your thoughts and intuition doesn't take a lot of time, though it can take a little planning, and it most certainly requires that you build up your spiritual muscle of contemplation and follow-through.

The first step is to begin acting on the small intuitive thoughts that float through your awareness. These take very little time or planning—they simply require that you pay attention and act on what you perceive. For instance, have you ever just gotten an intuitive hunch that the grocery store clerk would really benefit from a smile and your genuine inquiry about how her day is going? Have you noticed someone standing at a crosswalk and know, just by looking at them, that they're lost and could use some directions from a local resident? It's times like these to flex your spiritual muscle and act on what you think. For instance, smile at the clerk; give directions to the tourist.

Once you get a handle on these types of simple awareness and follow-through exercises, try challenging yourself to less-predictable situations. For example, you might one day have a pretty strong intuitive thought that you should carry a fire extinguisher in your car. There is no way to know if your thought is based on some future potential catastrophe, but it certainly couldn't hurt to have one in your car. Because you're paying attention to your intuitive hunches, you put one in the trunk and forget about it. Three weeks later, as you're loading a pile of groceries into your car, a sport utility vehicle drives into the parking lot with smoke seeping from its hood. The driver parks just beside you, pops the hood, and flames leap into the air. Fire extinguisher in hand, you save the day.

This scenario isn't so far-fetched. You're involved in conversations, activities, and events that may seem coincidental but actually are somehow interrelated to that innate sixth sense within you.

Cecelie was always one to follow her hunches and prepare for the seemingly unexpected. She lives in an area where a lot of small animals roam the streets, including her own pets. One day, Cecelie recognized a small voice within her that suggested it was dangerous for the animals to roam as they do. The next day, she left her own kitten inside when she went to the market. While there, she bought heavy waterproof gloves, trash bags, and collected some newspaper, and put them in the trunk of her car. On her way home that very afternoon, she drove by a sweet Siamese that had been hit on the road. By following through on her apparently random thoughts, Cecelie was prepared to gently and hygienically scoop the cat up and take it to the local pet emergency center, ultimately saving its life.

Situations like Cecelie's occur every day. If you pay attention to your thoughts and choose to follow through on at least a few of them, you'll recognize a growing wealth of spiritual currency accruing inside you. When you pay attention and follow through to what you intuit, you learn to recognize that coincidence doesn't really exist—events all are interrelated, always with specific purpose and meaning.

# Kick Off Your Shoes

From the time you wake up in the morning and place your bare feet on the throw rug by your bed, to when you finally kick off your snuggly slippers at night when you go to bed, your feet constantly are on the ground. In fact, the fifty-two bones in your feet are responsible for keeping you upright, supporting your spine, and carrying you from place to place—mostly without you giving them a second thought.

In many parts of the world, particularly in Asia and the Middle East, feet are revered and are perceived as windows of insight to health and healing. For thousands of years, in fact, the ancient, nonintrusive art of *reflexology* has been used to strengthen and promote physiological and spiritual changes in the body.

Reflexology is based on the premise that congestion or tension in any part of your foot mirrors congestion or tension in a corresponding part of your body. For example, tension in your big toes directly relates to tension in your head, which you may experience as a headache. The tips of all your other toes correspond to your sinuses; the heels of your feet directly correspond to your hips, lower lumbar, and sciatic nerve. In fact, all of your glands, organs, parts, and body systems directly correspond to specific areas on your feet. So, stimulating or massaging your whole foot has a relaxing and healing effect on your whole body.

Of course, you can treat your feet a little better by massaging them every once in a while, or by requesting that your sweetie rub your feet when you finally sit down at the end of the day. But often the very best of these types of intentions don't tend to last. Instead, why not choose to stimulate your soles by doing something you do every single day—WALK. The only twist is to walk on the uneven crust of the Earth without your shoes. That's right, you can experience the health benefits of sole stimulation by placing your bare feet on the ground and walking.

"Ouch!" you're thinking? Well, if you're careful and gentle, it doesn't hurt at all. In fact, walking barefoot on the ground will not only stimulate and encourage the healing of corresponding body parts but also make you feel more centered, grounded, and refreshed. Try it. You can begin on a soft surface such as grass and then slowly escalate your sole adventures to include dirt and even asphalt.

Joshua, a forty-two-year-old consultant, could barely believe he was going to hike through the forest without any shoes on, but his fiancée, Sabrina, was a member of the Barefoot Hiking Club (there are eight such clubs in the United States) and he wanted to experience the "tingling sensation" she always raved about. The only rule for the club was that everyone on the hike had to begin walking in bare feet. If you wanted, you could put on shoes after the first few strides, but people rarely did.

Joshua strapped his outdoor sandals to his belt and, with trepidation, started gingerly walking along the path barefoot. Sabrina was encouraging, reminding him that the first ten minutes were the most sensitive and then, almost magically, the uneven surface and stimulation would begin to feel good.

Surprisingly, Joshua began to enjoy himself even before the ten-minute span elapsed. At first he was focused step-by-step on where to place his tender feet; soon, he became aware that his sensitive soles began to adjust their pressure and gait all on their own. Instead of fixatedly gazing at the ground, Joshua relaxed and, for the first time, looked up at the breathtaking skyline view ahead of him. Not too long afterward, he noticed he was tingling. His whole body, just below the skin, felt like it was buzzing. His breath was easy. His laugh was bubbling. And his love for Sabrina was grand. His sandals didn't touch the ground once.

It's fun to walk barefoot. Don't you remember wanting to kick off your shoes and run through the sprinklers when you were a child? No one ever said that you have to always wear shoes when you're an adult.

The next time you're out in your yard, or at the park, or walking your dog, take off your shoes. Activate the bottoms of your feet against the Earth's surface, and enjoy the benefits of sole stimulation. You'll feel connected and young and vibrant. And you'll remember that the joys of childhood have great benefits (and are fun, too) well into your grown-up years.

# Touch the Environment

*We have not inherited the earth from our ancestors; we are borrowing it from our children.*

—A Native American wisdom saying

You don't have to "vote Green" or belong to a local environmental advocacy group to feel good about your contributions to the world. In fact, making the Earth a better place to live is a lot simpler, less time consuming, and abundantly more fun than you probably believe. More people than ever are conscious about recycling and reusing the products they buy. But what about participating in simple, fun ways to simultaneously help the environment and increase your fun quotient?

Here are some suggestions for having fun while becoming more spiritually aware of your environment:

**Go native:** Do you have a green thumb? Next time you're about to embark on reading a gardening magazine or planting seasonal flora, focus your attention on native plants, those that were growing in your hometown long before the first humans ever arrived.

Native plants are the foundation of the Earth's various ecosystems, or natural communities. They provide habitats and refuges for wildlife, especially birds. Native plants are beautiful and helpful in maintaining the health of the environment, and as an added benefit for being environmentally savvy, they're also easier and less expensive to care for. Once established, natives seldom need watering, mulching, or protection from the weather and pests, so they generally cost less to maintain over time.

**Watch birds:** Another avenue of ecological fun and contribution is to build a birdhouse or set up a birdbath in your yard or on your patio. Both help wildlife adapt to and survive the ever-increasing homes, people, and concrete overtaking their natural habitats. For added fun, buy or borrow from the library a bird book so that you can observe, track, and record the birds that regularly visit.

**Care about animals:** If wild plants and birds aren't your thing, what about increasing your awareness around what domestic animals in your local area may need? You can offer to pet sit a cat while your neighbors are away (it requires only ten or so minutes a day), or volunteer to periodically walk a dog for an elderly or sick neighbor (again, just a ten-minute investment). Abandoned pets are a big problem in many communities. If you don't have time to volunteer at a local animal shelter, it can be just as beneficial for you to forward to animal agencies relevant research, program ideas, and personnel information you read online or in a magazine.

**Pick up trash:** You've heard it before, probably ever since childhood. "Pick up the trash." Not only yours, but someone else's, too. It doesn't take a gargantuan effort, simply bend down and pick up litter. Whether it's in the street, at the playground, or blown into your neighbor's drive, pick it up and throw it away.

**Use nature's products:** Make holiday cards on tree bark; make gifts for friends using leaves, seashells, sticks, rocks, etc. The more you delve into natural creativity, the more you help the environment while having fun and feeling good.

**Support what's good:** Be aware of what you buy, both in terms of the products you purchase and the companies that produce them. For example, be careful to buy goods that are created from recycled or natural products, and invest money in ecologically sound funds where you simultaneously make money and feel good about supporting the planet.

The results of touching the environment a little more frequently, with a little more awareness and increased fun, will amaze you. It's all simple effective enjoyment with everlasting benefit. To affect the world, you don't have to change your vote, be a liberal, or eat exclusively vegetables—you need only commit to having fun, with a little conscientiousness.

# Refresh Your Habits

Have you been doing and saying some things for so long that you aren't even aware you're doing them anymore? If you're like most of us, your life is unknowingly anesthetized with habitual behaviors. Although most habits originally are initiated because they are effective, eventually they exist as a matter of rote. Arguably, habits contribute to your productivity, but, if you're unaware, they simultaneously can cause spiritual narcolepsy.

You get used to doing things a certain way because you rely on routine and stability to decrease your stress and increase your efficiency. Nine times out of ten, habits allow you to know what to expect, how to act, and on what you can rely. But soon enough, habits can cause the exact limitations they were born to dispel.

Whether it's a word, an activity, or a deed, your habits are only good for as long as they help you. Unless you can keep them fresh, they're simply limiting. Contrary to what you may believe, minor habitual behavior isn't too difficult to change. Sometimes, as you'll see, it's as simple as whether or not to wear a watch.

Toni, for example, had been a "watch person" ever since she graduated from college and entered the corporate world of business. Knowing the time was imperative to Toni's success and, before long, it was second nature to her to tilt her wrist and quickly glance at the time. Not only were her watches fashion statements but she also relied on them to keep her on time, stable, productive, and effective.

After five years of a high-stress, seventy-hour-a-week career, Toni quit her job to pursue her self-employment dreams. In honor of her new commitment, she took off her watch and swore not to wear one ever again. Toni discovered a newfound level of freedom in not knowing exactly what time it was. When she needed to know the time, she simply asked someone. Releasing the habit of continual time keeping was challenging, but freeing.

Nearly ten years later, self-employed and successful, Toni joined a community tennis team. She had so much fun on the courts that she often would lose track of time, which unfortunately threw off her entire day's schedule. For the first time in a decade, Toni missed wearing a watch.

Though at first she promised herself she'd only wear it on the courts, Toni was astonished at how much freedom and less stress she felt from knowing exactly what time it was. How interesting it was that the exact feelings she had when she took off her watch ten years earlier were the same feelings she experienced when she started to wear it again.

Just for fun, try consciously to change just one of your habitual behaviors. Don't pick a difficult one that will be too challenging to accomplish. Choose one that is simple, but significant.

❖ If you wear a watch, take it off; if you don't wear a watch, begin to wear one. The same goes for hats, jewelry, and other, similar items—if you do something, stop doing it. If you don't do something, try it out for a while.

❖ If a vase has been sitting on your dining room table for years, move it to another location.

❖ If you typically pack a sack lunch in the morning to take to the office, try packing it before you go to sleep the previous evening.

❖ If you usually take your dog for a walk counterclockwise around the neighborhood, try walking it in the opposite direction.

❖ If you usually stroke your chin while being pensive, try running your hand through your hair instead.

There is a freedom and beauty to changing your habits. Refreshing your environment and enlivening your habitual behaviors will color excitement, freedom, and creativity into your everyday actions, and it will naturally revive your awareness as well. Give it try.

# Walking in the Woods

We live in a world that often seems dead, or at least without feeling. Civilization is essentially a mechanical insight. It views the universe as a mechanical device—as a machine, rather than as a body. This way of viewing the world around us has an enormous impact on how we view each other and how we act toward each other.

People are used to thinking of stones and dirt as unliving objects, and trees as simple, insensate creations. We are all aware of the tendency toward placing a monetary value on things. A type of valuing that sometimes supersedes all other possible valuations or worth.

Yet our lives consist of constant interaction with objects. Things define us because we live in a universe that is concrete and real. Our senses react to the smell and the touch of the world, and this is very precious.

The physical world casts its aura upon us and we are never free from it. Nor should we be. Being surrounded by objects, animate and inanimate, and our way of viewing them define our entire existence.

Children are great teachers in this regard because they tend to live more in the body than adults and to be more aware of their physical surroundings than the grown-ups.

Eli, a thirteen-year-old girl, for example, is a great one for the outdoors and for hiking in the woods. She is always suggesting that her family troop through this or that forest—the further away from home and the more exotic, the better. Her purpose is not directed toward any destination really, nor does the hiking have a purpose in any material sense. It is just the pleasure of the world. It is just the pleasure of being there.

We need nature as a part of our inner landscape. We need to constantly reacquaint ourselves with the objects that surround us. Eli's home was in a hilly area near town. The area recently had been built up but still retained patches of scrub pine, eucalyptus, and wild rose. Walking in the neighborhood was a fragrant and green experience. The pine mixed with the eucalyptus for a slightly intoxicating outdoor smell. But when Eli walked with her father, she noticed he was not really paying much attention. He was anxious to get home and resume work that he needed to do.

"It's time to go," he said.

"No hurry," she replied.

"Yes it *is* time to go," he said, more sternly.

"The forest isn't in a hurry," she said.

"True," he replied, "but perhaps the forest doesn't care."

"Wrong," she said. "The forest's whole life is care."

Eli's father stopped and thought about this. He wasn't exactly sure what she meant, nor was he even sure she could explain what she meant. But the implication was, for him, very revealing. "The forest's whole life is care."

"All right," he said, "fair enough. If the forest cares so much about us, I guess it's only right that we go on to the end."

This satisfied her and they hiked till the dusk came and the night bats began to flit through the branches.

Take a day or a weekend (if you have the time), and consciously treat everything as if it were alive. Whether you are in the forest or driving in traffic, try to see each thing as if it had a soul and were worthy of respect. Even the parking meter—even the parking meter attendant! Before you use something for your own pleasure or in a utilitarian way, ask its permission, or explain with a word or two why you are using it.

This will almost certainly feel very silly for a little while, but the benefits are great. When we treat objects as if they were only there for our use and pleasure, before very long we begin to treat people in the same way.

The truth is, every object has its reason and its use. This reason of being has very little to do with us. We are well served never to forget this.

---

# Don't Save It for Later

Delayed gratification is overrated. If you're a responsible adult living in the twenty-first century, putting off for later what you can exquisitely enjoy right now is a bit ludicrous. Lives have never been busier. As long as you're taking care of your commitments—such as paying your bills, spending time with those you love, and other similar responsibilities—you should allow yourself to indulge in enjoyment every possible time it arises.

Delayed gratification must have its roots in the Depression era, when people lost everything or had so little that they began to save—and sometimes to hoard—their belongings and experiences. "In case of emergency" was synonymous with resilience.

In today's world, delaying for later what you can enjoy now is a surefire recipe for discontent. Life today is busy. Commitments, social engagements, and professional obligations take up the majority of your time. When a little piece of grace slips into your day, don't save it for later—seize it immediately.

It's important to plan for the future; it's also essential to enjoy yourself. If you're not careful, there can be little difference between accumulation and deprivation. If you're always saving something until later, you might never be able to enjoy it because later may never come.

The Buddha said, "Death is more certain than tomorrow." To some, this may sound like a fatalistic philosophy. In fact, it's the opposite. Consistently staying aware of life's beauty, magnificence, and opportunity allows us to enjoy each moment we're alive. Your life can disappear in less than a breath—and it can continue forever. Under these circumstances, why would you want to put off for a moment what you could appreciate and enjoy now?

Joel had been practicing mindfulness meditation for more than a decade. Still, with all his training and ability to stay present, he always failed to apply his skills to "in-the-moment" enjoyment. He had learned from a young age that if you save something, it had more meaning. So, although Joel was able to stay emotionally available to moment-by-moment events, he rarely chose to immediately and actively indulge in pure enjoyment.

For example, whenever Joel received cards in the mail, he'd set them aside to read later, at a time he felt would be most appropriate and more enjoyable. As a result, he sometimes completely missed events, purely because the "right moment" hadn't arrived for him to read the invitations.

At a restaurant one evening, Joel's friend Brian ordered dessert first, specifically asking that it be brought to him at the beginning of the meal. When the dessert arrived at the same time as Joel's hot and sour soup, he was shocked.

"What are you doing?" Joel asked. His friend explained that he loved eating mango and sticky rice at Thai restaurants, but if he waited to order it for dessert, he was always too full.

What is the point of always waiting until later? As long as you know the essential facts to keep you healthy and safe, what could be more beneficial than first doing what you enjoy and then taking care of the rest? You deserve to enjoy yourself now, when you have the time for it.

If you stockpile your happiness, you may just never have a chance to experience it. For example, if you spend most weeks of the year working overtime so you can later take an extended holiday, it might not happen as you planned. Your body and mind may be so overworked and exhausted that you'll spend equal time recuperating on your vacation as you do enjoying yourself.

Whether it's taking a break in the middle of the afternoon to enjoy the surprise of an early spring day or ordering dessert first, upping your enjoyment quota is essential. Of course, you can't be crazy and indulge yourself at the expense of your health, security, or family. You might enjoy yourself more if you save something for later. Most likely, though, that's just a habitual belief that you can easily shift.

Revel in your moments—they're precious. Believe that now is the right time to enjoy yourself. Don't save your enjoyment for later, for more of it most certainly will be available then, too.

# Shake Routines into the Present

When you eat breakfast, do you even taste the fresh fruit you're swallowing? Have you looked out the window even once to see what kind of day it is? Chances are, if you're like most of us, you spend one-third of your waking hours at work, one-third taking care of yourself, your family, and your home, and one-third trying to do everything else. With all of these demands, how can you possibly manage your time effectively and reserve enough energy to stay aware and be present? It can be difficult.

To effectively "do it all," you've probably fallen into the comfort of routine. And why not? Routines let you effectively accomplish lots of activities in short periods of time. The downside is that routines are mind numbing. Most people go through their mornings—perhaps even days, weeks, or months, heaven forbid—without noticing the freshness of a day.

Each spring, Jerry and his wife, Cindy, make jars and jars of strawberry jam from the fruit in their garden. At first, each bite of jelly-smeared toast tastes more appetizing than the last. The sweet taste and smell of strawberries fill Jerry with the exquisite nourishment, love, and accomplishment that only homemade jam can provide. Mornings in the springtime motivates Jerry to wake up just a little earlier so he has the time to linger over his breakfast. Somehow by the winter, though, Jerry barely finds the time to brush his teeth in the morning—let alone have an enjoyable meal. Instead, he'll slap his coveted jam onto slightly burnt toast and cram it down as he backs the car out of the driveway. Whoa—Jerry, what happened?

It's times like this—and even at less obvious warning flags—that you have to shake yourself out of possible rote behaviors and change the way you do your everyday activities. You don't have to do anything dramatic; just slightly change situations so that you can't take them for granted.

Here are some routine-rearranging options:

❖ **Change the order or the ingredients of your mornings.** If you're used to waking up, showering, dressing, and then having breakfast—rearrange the order of your activities. For instance, wake up, eat breakfast, make your lunch, then shower and dress. Or, if you're used to having coffee every morning, try a cup of tea or orange juice instead. Trade cereal for cottage cheese. Scrambled eggs for two eggs over easy. You get the idea.

❖ **Reorganize the drawers in your bureau or rearrange your closet.** It doesn't take much effort to switch your T-shirt drawer with your pants drawer. Or to move all your shirts to the other side of the closet. In fact, it's simple. Yet it will stir you up, just for a second, bringing you right into the present moment. Be sure to laugh at yourself—or at least silently chuckle—each time you routinely open the wrong drawer or reach into the wrong side of the closet, and then pause, and appreciate your presence. You easily can try this exercise in the kitchen as well. The next time you empty your dishwasher, put your coffee or tea mugs where your glasses usually go. It isn't a gargantuan effort, but it will refresh your routine.

❖ **Reset your car radio stations.** Oh no, not the radio, you say. But think about it, for how long have you been listening to the same radio stations? When is the last time you listened to a brand-new radio station—one on which you don't automatically know what music will be played, what the DJs will say, or what commercials will try to seduce you? Who knows, maybe your tastes have changed. Start at the bottom of the dial and push the "seek" button on your car radio. When you hear music you like, pause and listen. If the radio station plays two songs in a row that you enjoy, recognize, or simply like the beat of, push the "set" button. In no time at all you'll have a whole new repertoire of musical selections.

You'll be surprised at the fresh enjoyment you'll receive from creating a bit of newness in your days. It's not so difficult; and, honestly, it can even be kind of funny—who would ever have imagined you actually liked classical music or talk radio? Who would have believed that you had time to sit down for breakfast before jumping in the shower?

These moments of awareness are a gift. They're an opportunity to appreciate what is simple, to remember who you are, to joyfully laugh at how you live. Shaking your routines into the present provides just the flash you need to be in the here and now. Stop doing everything the way you always do it. Change the order of things; gently shake yourself up a bit.

# Nearly Effortless Effect

Making someone else feel good makes you feel good. It's a simple fact of life. But you're busy. We all are. You have so much to do and accomplish that finding volunteer time can become just another thing on the to-do list that pushes you over the edge, throws you off balance, and maybe even creates resentment.

In truth, volunteering can take a lot of time. Contrary to what you may believe, however, you still can feel great helping others without it costing you a lot of time or money. If you can't spare the time, you don't have to volunteer for half a day to make phone calls during a fund-raising event; you don't have to spend time weekly with a special needs child if you already spend hours a day with your own or someone else's children; nor must you donate large sums of money to your favorite charities, especially if you're already on a tight budget. Of course, if you have the time or finances, all of these activities help others tremendously. Keep in mind, however, there are many little things you can choose to do that are nearly effortless and still contribute significantly to bettering someone else's life.

Here's a sample of activities for you to consider doing. Although none of them requires much of your time or money, they most assuredly will increase your philanthropic contributions, enhancing how you feel about yourself and significantly making the lives of others healthier, happier, and more comfortable.

**Collect toiletries:** The next time you're staying in a hotel that provides complimentary shampoo, conditioner, soap, shower caps, shoe buffer, etc., throw the extras into your bag. When you get home from your trip, drive by your local shelter and drop off the gift package for individuals who need it. Good for you!

**Pick up litter:** Cleaning up your environment can be as simple as picking up (instead of stepping over) the discarded bottle on the sidewalk, the fast-food bag near the park bench, or the soda can lodged into the sand at the beach. Most trash isn't goopy with crud and won't make your hands smell, so picking it up and tossing it into the next available receptacle is simple and makes the environment more beautiful for the next person. Good job!

**Help clean up:** Any small organization, synagogue, bookstore, or community center that hosts speakers or events needs help cleaning up. You may not have the time to stay for fifteen minutes to straighten up the entire room, but you certainly have an extra five seconds to move your chair to the side or put it in the storage closet. It will be a great help to others, and you may even receive an appreciative smile from the event coordinator. Way to go!

**Give your stuff away:** You probably have a bunch of stuff that you don't use that other people would greatly appreciate having. Think about your closets, storage areas, basements, maybe even the corner of your office or under your child's bed. What is there that you don't need that others could use? Maybe you have old toys, winter coats, clothes, old appliances, outdated computers, books, magazines, etc. All these things can be such great contributions for others. Pack them up and take them over to a homeless shelter, a library, or a children's hospital. You don't have to make a big project out of it. You can do it a little at a time. Some organizations will even come and pick up the donation right from your driveway. How thoughtful of you!

**Take a goodie bag with you when you leave a restaurant:** Your leftovers are an entire meal for a homeless person. When you're done eating, ask for a to-go container for your leftover grilled vegetables and chicken, or even just the complimentary bread from the table. (Don't forget a plastic fork and a napkin!) If you live in a city where you walk by homeless people, personally hand the meal to them and smile. How generous (and delicious)!

As you can see, it doesn't take a lot of effort to have a lot of effect. Just a little extra thought and a teensy bit of effort will make all the difference in the world.

# Again and Again and Again

Besides eating and drinking, can you name one thing you do 365 days of the year? Is there a single thing you make it a point to do every single day?

It isn't surprising that people's days are overflowing with a slew of activities, but it's shocking that so few—if any—are repeated on a daily basis. With the exception of bathing or brushing teeth, most days are filled with unrelated activities strung together one right after the next. This may be okay for some, but for people trying to bring a little more sanity into their lives, a consistent, reliable activity may be just the key, and it could increase their health as well.

Kilbur was a successful gardener who spent most of his time hurriedly rushing from one client's home to the next. Not surprisingly, his bad back, which had been a problem for years, had started to go numb from increased pressure on a pinched nerve.

"Have you tried walking every day?" a nurse asked him on one of his infrequent trips to the doctor. "If you walk every day, something will change and you'll experience relief, I promise."

Kilbur thought the nurse was ridiculous. Who ever heard of such a thing? Besides, he was outside and physically active six out of seven days. Although the thought of doing extra exercise was practically ludicrous, Kilbur thought he'd try it in lieu of taking the prescription painkillers that made him too drowsy to keep up with work. So, every day after work, Kilbur walked for twenty minutes. Regardless of the season or the weather or his mood, he walked every single day. Sometimes he walked quickly. Sometimes he barely ambled. The benefits were slow to come, but they were steady. Before long, Kilbur found himself feeling a whole lot better, laughing more easily, and being less judgmental and cranky.

Kilbur never claimed that walking was what made his back and his life dramatically improve. He became a huge advocate, however, for choosing to do a daily activity.

Whether you choose to exercise each day or to simply sit down and breathe for a few minutes, having a daily commitment will bring you back to your core. Day after day, it will stay consistent, reminding you that no matter what happens in any twenty-four-hour period, a certain part of you always will show up and deal with whatever life has to offer.

The key to effectiveness is everyday consistency. Choose an activity that takes little time and is simple to accomplish. Select a specific amount of time—one month to one year—in which you are committed to doing the activity every single day of your life, no matter what.

Don't be extravagant in your choosing, and if you need support to help you accomplish your goal, be sure to ask for it. Jill, a beginning meditator, wanted to sit mindfully on her meditation cushion every day for one month and then, if she liked the results, she would commit for one year to sit every single day. She chose to sit for ten minutes, which seemed to her easy enough to accomplish. To help her out, she requested that her partner, Peter, encourage her to sit before they went to bed if she hadn't already done so earlier in the day. Ten minutes? Who can honestly say that they can't find a spare ten minutes in their days?

Besides sitting and walking, other daily activities that can be accomplished in a set period of time can include:

❖ Telling your partner or your children that you love them and why

❖ Reading poetry

❖ Writing in your journal

❖ Dancing in your living room

You get the idea. Your options for a daily activity are limitless. Be creative. Although there probably isn't one activity that you would enjoy doing every single day, you can most definitely choose one that you'll enjoy doing most of the time—and on the other days, do it anyway.

# PART IV

## Be It

# Mundane Moments of Grandeur

A person's life does not consist only of great moments. Even a hero or role model, whose life seems to be made of the stuff of history, in reality moves through existence simply—their life consisting of thousands of simple moments: driving the car, making toast, reading the paper, washing underwear.

A life of only extreme moments would soon become hell. If each moment were lived in extremity, whether good or bad, we would soon expire from the exertion. For there to be the out breath, there must be an in breath. Always, life is balanced. Without this, it would become intolerable.

Though you easily can see the ecstatic instant of a blossom, there must be steady soil to support the growing rose. That is, there must be an inner tranquillity of spirit to support your explosive insights. At the same time, each moment is meant to be a small, exquisite jewel—but just for a moment. Each moment is counted and countable. Each can be touched and felt, like a finger running over a piece of porcelain.

Each moment is a great opportunity of spirit. An opportunity, of a sort, no matter how simple, that will never be seen again. Never mind that it is not an ecstatic moment. It can be quite a perfect moment. This is far more important really, far more perfect. For each moment is a moment of you. That is, each specific moment is the sum definition of who you are at that specific place in time.

For Nancy there were few things in life she found more annoying or fatiguing than cleaning. The worst type of cleaning by far was cleaning her room. Her mother used to say: "A place for everything and everything in its place." God, how she hated that phrase. It seemed like she had heard it every day of her life! But, in reflection, she did have to admit that things tended to pile up. She sat on her bed looking over the disarray of her room. It was a veritable Niagara Falls of stuff; an overwhelming flood of objects that were ankle deep. "It is a pigsty," she said to herself and began slowly bending down, picking things up, and putting them away.

This time, however, while she was picking up her items, she found herself falling into a new mental pattern. Instead of trying to rush through everything, she deliberately slowed herself down and lingered over many of the objects. She found herself reminiscing about the items and pieces of clothing, gazing and holding things that she had not seen for a while. At the same time, she began to realize that some of the things were fine to let go of and give away, and others she would cherish a bit more.

A couple of hours passed. They passed very quickly and Nancy was surprised when she looked at the clock. What had made the difference in the passing of time? It was immediately apparent that it was not what she did, but how she did it. How she experienced cleaning depended completely on who she was in the moment of cleaning.

To learn how to be fully present in your moments, try the following exercise: Find twenty minutes a day to clean something that you aren't normally involved with in a cleaning sort of way. Use the cleaning time as a meditation. Remember, everything ultimately is a meditation because it is meant to engage you in a true and honest way. Try and linger over what you are doing. If it is a dust pile or cobweb, take just a moment and see it. Nothing may come to the mind, which is fine, or an insight may arise. The point is just changing the focus of your action—be more in the moment. Allow the connotations of each object to linger for a moment on the mind, rather than rushing through your actions without attention.

You may get less done in the short run, but the long run will become ever so much more enjoyable and nourishing.

# Take an Extra Breath

Breathing is simple. It's natural. In fact, in most cases you don't have to do anything to breathe. Typically, you inhale 21 times a minute, 30,240 times a day—all without giving your breath a second thought. Maybe after running up a flight of stairs or trying to catch a train you'll notice your breathing. But, in most cases, your breath is part of a perfect, divinely inspired autonomic nervous system, flawlessly functioning all on its own.

Many spiritual traditions and ancient teachings focus on breathing techniques as a gateway to increased awareness and better health. These methods may seem overly complicated or weird, and reaping their benefits oftentimes requires the patience and perseverance of a long-term practice. In lieu of this, the simplest approach is to just pay attention to your natural breath. And, in those cases when your natural breath is either more stifled or excited than usual, taking an "extra" breath makes all the difference in the world.

What would happen if you actually paid attention to your breathing? By minding your breath—for just seconds at a time—your perspective and understanding of situations exponentially increases. Once a day, for four to five inhalations, bring your attention exclusively to your breath and breathe. Notice how paying attention to your breath immediately calms you. Breathing in consciously and then exhaling with attention allows you to recognize what truthfully is happening in the moment versus becoming caught in what you fear the moment may be.

When the phone rang at 6:45 A.M., Faith's heart skipped a beat. When she picked up the phone and heard her father's voice cracking on the other end, Faith's breath nearly disappeared altogether. What could be wrong? It had to be about her mother.

In between the gasps of her father's bated breath, Faith heard him say, "It's your mother, Faith. Oh, my goodness, your mother . . ."

The surge of pain in Faith's chest nearly knocked her over. Breathe, she thought. Focus your attention on your breath and breathe. Pause, she told herself. Consciously breathe in; consciously exhale. Focus on your breath and don't assume what has happened or how to respond.

"What's up, Pop?" Another breath.

"It's your mother," he exclaimed, "she's just been honored as the 'Best New Sculptor' in the entire country. We're so excited."

Ah, the fear was unfounded: the news is good. Faith took another breath, this time one filled with relief. Thank goodness.

All you need to remember is to pay attention to your breath when you're most likely to forget about it altogether. It's not so far-fetched to claim that entire histories could be rewritten if only people remembered to breathe. Forgetting to breathe causes entire situations to be missed, misinterpreted, or permanently altered.

The next time your heart rate increases, for whatever reason, and hence your breathing quickens, your job is to be sure not only of your breathing but also that you take an *extra* breath. Don't form any opinions until you've successfully brought your attention to your breathing. Whether it's that your partner has for the first time said, "I love you," or your boss has said she expected more results from a project you're working on, or your mother asks you for the umpteenth time why you never tell her anything, allow those initial moments to pass without response or definition.

One extra breath—consciously inhaling and exhaling—provides the necessary space for your reaction to accurately ripen. It allows the moment to truly express itself and, in the process, allows you to see, and understand, and respond. One extra breath can calm your heart, turning a reaction into an appropriate response. Who knows, that extra air may even create space for you to learn, hear, or see something you never before even imagined.

# Save Your Opinions for Later

How can you distinguish what you know from what you think you know? How do you realize, in the heat of an experience, for instance, whether what you are feeling is based on present-day circumstances or the fear of history repeating itself?

Most of us think we know what is happening, how we are feeling, and what we are doing. And, in truth, we probably do—to some degree. Though, for every angle that you understand, there is another angle that you barely fathom at all.

More people than ever before devote a considerable amount of their income to seeing a therapist, exercising, receiving a massage, attending retreats—all with the intention of becoming more developed and aware. Though all these things help us better understand our families, our situations, and ourselves, we can sometimes become so lost in what we believe we've learned that we can completely miss the opportunity to experience the freshness of a situation.

For Jodi, having an opinion—or choosing not to have one—became especially relevant in a fateful conversation she had one morning with her dear friend Tracey. As soon as she answered the phone, Tracey's familiar giggle alerted Jodi that a man was in the same room as her friend.

"Oh," Jodi said, "you have a man in your house?"

Intuitively, Jodi knew that the man was Tracey's ex-boyfriend, Dan; someone with whom Tracey had been trying to be "just friends" with for quite some time.

"It's Dan," Tracey proclaimed in apparent joy. "And guess what else? We're getting married!"

Jodi couldn't imagine how Tracey had so rapidly come to the decision not only to take up her difficult relationship with Dan but also to marry him. In a flood of emotion, Jodi had a choice: she could hold tight to her personal opinions and state aloud what she *thought* was best for her friend, or she could choose to breathe into the moment to create a space in her heart and in her mind that allowed and supported Tracey to be exactly who she was. Jodi reminded herself that she doesn't always know what is best for herself, let alone for anyone else. She chose not to form any personal opinions about her friend's choices until she had more information.

No one other than Tracey and Dan (who soon will be celebrating their twenty-second wedding anniversary) could possibly have known that what they needed most was a deeper commitment, not separation. By embracing their fears and stepping firmly into love, their actions insisted that they—and their friends—not predetermine the supposed outcome of a situation.

The next time you believe a situation is "all wrong" or "all right," try holding off forming an opinion at all. Certainly you should honor any hunches you may have; however, whenever you think you *absolutely* know something, it's the best indication that you may know nothing at all. In fact, the strongest of opinions most often and most severely limits opportunities.

Here's what you can keep in mind:

❖ First, as soon as you realize you have an opinion, clearly state to yourself what that opinion is. You can do this by mentally acknowledging the opinion or writing it down.

❖ Next, take at least one deep breath. If you have the patience, take three deep breaths. Tell yourself that you are willing to learn from the experience. That although it feels familiar and you believe you may already know the outcome, you are willing to not know.

❖ Take another breath, and continue to pay attention to your thoughts, though do not allow them to lead you anywhere specific.

In due time, you'll know if your initial opinion was accurate for the particular circumstance. And quite often, it may have been. At least as often, however, you'll be surprised at what you learn from postponing your opinions. It creates a sense of appreciation for the unique; it subtly though powerfully teaches the art of humility and respect.

# Measuring Time

How do we measure time? Each person measures time differently. How you measure time reveals a lot about you and helps define how you move through the day. Time is one of the eyes through which we view reality.

Most people define time by their watches, but of course this is not the only way. Some, more leisured types of individuals measure time by the cups of coffee they consume. Some tribal folk who still move more slowly through the day and, by American standards, seem caught out of time, perhaps still measure time by the movement of the sun. Some people (mostly those who don't live in urban settings) measure time by mood, or the simple duration of a job and their fatigue level.

But most people wear a watch. One friend has a little button on the side of his watch—if you push it, the face lights up. He says he likes it because when he wakes up in the middle of the night, he can see what time it is. This habitual behavior soothes him and makes it easier to go back to sleep. What does this say about him?

Every culture and each individual has a specific relationship with time and its passage. Think for a moment, How do you measure time? What are the ways in which you check in with the movement of life? Do you think of time as your friend or as an enemy—or is it simply something neutral?

These days, people tend to measure time in ever smaller increments. Historically, this has been a trend. As technology has grown and become increasingly important, time has become more divided and subtle. There was quite a cultural crisis when clocks first appeared. Think how your life would be different if you thought of time in large chunks rather than small. What if you referred to time in terms such as "morning," "noonish," "afternoon," "evening," and "night." A friend would ask, "When do you want to get together?" And you would reply, "Hmmm, morning."

Think if your office ran like this. How about the world? The clock has shaped civilizations as well as each of our individual lives. As the clock has steadily measured increasing subtleties of time, so have people tried to adhere and model themselves to these finer distinctions. Modern-day society has tried to capture, with excruciating levels of exactitude, the minute changes of time: to be aware of them; to own them; even, ultimately, to be them.

It is a wonderful exercise to attempt to change your sense of time. Try for a few minutes to recapture the sense of timelessness you experienced as a child. Children don't inhabit the same kind of time link to the world as grown-ups do. Time, for children, is not fine-tuned. Instead, their sense of time is "right now!" or "don't care." Once their sense of time does set in place, though, it is almost as deep as potty training.

A good exercise is to take a few days and consciously try and change your whole time sense. Pick a weekend, from Friday night until Sunday evening, to put away your watch and cover the clocks in your house. Move according to the rhythms of the sun and the needs of your friends and family. Move according to your mood. The inner clock of your nature is something you most likely take very little accounting of, but it belongs to your most primordial aspect. It is one of the building blocks of your very being. To get in touch with it, even for a very limited time, is a gift. The birds awaken early, some animals late—see how you feel about such a schedule, but feel it internally. Fight the temptation to pick up the watch, and simply move through the day.

It is fine to set your mind on taking care of chores, but plan for them, not by the clock but by your own sense of: "Now it's time to go to the bank," and "Now I'm hungry, I think I'll eat a slice of pizza," and so on. It goes deeper than mere mood; it begins to reflect your entire relationship with the world. As such, it is extraordinarily useful. The shifting that will occur even after only a couple of days of such a self-imposed change will be timelessly illuminating.

# The Wisdom of Boredom

We have forgotten how to be bored. It is a pejorative word these days. Heaven forbid a person should be bored! We spend enormous amounts of time, money, and of course energy being sure we are not bored, even for a moment. Boredom has had whole industries invented to keep it at bay.

But there is wisdom in boredom that should not be overlooked. For in those moments when we feel stuck and there is nothing to do, we simultaneously begin to inhabit a world that is illuminating in a very different sort of way than anything else that we experience in our busy, busy lives. In those times when there is nothing "to do," we are stuck with ourselves, and this offers us great insight and opportunity. Our minds are filled with the "white noise" of our busy lives. But when we can turn our inner eye upon ourselves, a great garden becomes visible. And this garden becomes visible only within the moment of inner quiet, a quiet that, for most of us, is defined as boredom.

Truly, in the final analysis, we are our own most interesting subject. Remember it is only through our own perception that all understanding must inevitably come.

Harry was driving halfway across the state for a meeting with some investors. It was a long drive, but the distance really wasn't great enough to merit a plane flight. Halfway there, his car broke down. He found himself in a little town far from anywhere. It consisted of a main street two blocks long, crossed by a street that was not even paved.

There was one gas station and the mechanic there told him the car needed a common part, but it could not be gotten for at least two days, which was the same amount of time it would take for the bus to come through. There was nothing remotely like a taxi service and his company was not interested in sending a driver. In short, he was stuck. He raged and raved in exasperation. He called his wife at home and repeatedly called and berated his office. But there was nothing they could do. He considered (briefly) buying a whole new car. But ultimately, there was just nothing to be done. So, for the first time in many years, he was stuck in a place with few amenities for passing time. There was a café, but no movie theater and no television in his hotel.

As time passed he began to alternate between manic energy and lassitude. But as more time passed, and he had explored the main street (all two blocks of it) for the twentieth time, his own internal clock began to slow down. By the end of his imposed virtual retreat, he had begun to see his experience a little differently.

Boredom can be very awkward. When we are stuck with ourselves, there is no one else to blame or dramatize about. We realize a great truth—we are the universe written small; in other words, ultimately all interest and meaning are gained through the clearinghouse of our own perception and understanding.

Part of our apparent quest as modern people (and no less in Third World nations desperate to take on all the toys of technology) is to create toys that fill our minds so much that there is no time for self. An exercise of great preciousness is to create a zone of time, a temporary place situated in time where we act differently; a context that shapes us, even if we are tired or distracted. It moves us in a certain direction, inexorably.

Creating such a zone of time and space—a ritualized period of time—permits time to act upon our hearts. A wonderful time already given to us is the Sabbath—a twenty-hour period of time to relax, to reconnect, to enjoy the simplicity of doing nothing ordinary. People have forgotten about the vast wisdom of the Sabbath peace, but it resides directly in boredom. For in that space there is only our own still, small voice. When boredom is embraced, it transforms us. We begin to see the startling possibilities that lie scattered about us. Then, even more startlingly, we begin to see who we are.

# Celebration Contemplation

People talk a lot about becoming aware and developing insight. But you have to ask yourself —aware of what? Insight to what? It is often said: "Just be aware of what 'is.'" This sounds nice, but still, what is the "is"?

Each moment in your life is trying to bloom; yet, unless you are willing to let it, it can't. Too much analyzing of the awareness of the moment kills it. Natural spontaneity is the ticket. It's not a matter of just being yourself, it's a matter of being your deeper self: playful, crazy, only sometimes logical, and most of all having a good time. These intentions reflect more than just humanity—all of creation works this way. Or at least wants to.

Making your life a celebration of contemplation—a celebration of life—is not always easy, but certainly it is attractive. Imagine living each moment (or trying to) as if life were a miracle, and as if each hour and minute of life were breathless with stunning potential.

It might sound airy-fairy, but it's easier than you think. Contemplative celebration involves making yourself the conduit of/for joy, and in the process releasing the joy that is inherent in you and resides in every person. It's a matter of choice and action. Choosing to observe life's adventures from a place of spontaneity, fun, and positivity, and then celebrating those observations by acting from your heart. Contemplative celebration is enjoyable—it's the cause of smiles that bubble up from a place deep inside of you.

Acts of celebration contemplation include leaving messages on your door designed to cheer up the postman; delivering cookies to your coworkers for no other reason than it's a Wednesday; performing scenes from Shakespeare (with liberal ad lib) on street corners, in cafés, on the bus; painting flowers on your outdoor trash cans; leaving money (rather small amounts are fine) tacked up on public billboards.

George, a financially successful though unhappy young man, often ate dinner out alone. One evening, the waiter asked how George had enjoyed the food. He replied: "I was very unhappy for two reasons: First, the food was awful. I could hardly eat a bite. Second, the portions were so small!"

The contradiction in George's words might make you laugh. But this is how some people approach life. The food is awful, and why are the portions so small? We may complain about the inadequacies of our world, but really what we want to do is soak up everything and experience as much as we can. In reality, the food is great and the portions more than ample. If you allow your life to be a feast, you can celebrate every day.

As an exercise, take on the task to eradicate simple conformity in your life for a set period, perhaps five days. As part of this practice, actively decide to embrace joy as a legitimate method for your spiritual practice and endeavor. Though the world may have great suffering, it is in essence a place of celebration. During these five days, see your life through the looking glass of celebration contemplation. Do everything you can to celebrate, but keep each celebration simple: leave strange telephone messages on your machine; nickname people with love; talk a lot with strangers.

Let your heart be your guide. Let inner celebration be your truest contemplation.

# The Gentle Art of Puttering

There is a lot of talk these days about the need for serious meditation. As more people complain of being too busy and too frantic, meditation is trumpeted from every billboard as the answer. But the truth is, we have been reaping the benefits of meditating for a long, long time—it's not a new practice. It has existed, but it has had a very homespun quality to it in the past with a very simple, homespun name: puttering. The art of puttering sprang from the same ancient origins of meditation.

Eric's first recollection of this art in practice came when he was about six. As a sometimes rambunctious kid, and an only child, Eric was regularly dropped off at the large, old, rather musty Victorian home of his grandaunts, Minnie and Thelma, in hope that they could keep track of him. Neither of his aunts would ever see the sunny side of seventy again, but they kept active. They were never in a hurry and it was the family hope that their slow and steady ways would serve to calm young Eric down, at least to a manageable degree.

When Eric arrived, he was eager to play or go somewhere (it hardly mattered where), but Minnie insisted that he simply follow her about the house as she did chores. He was aghast. "Just follow you around?" he said. It sounded like torture.

"Oh, it won't be so bad," she laughed and off she set.

At first these chores did seem like torture and interminable to boot. Because instead of just going and doing whatever it was she needed to do, she would do things around it and then eventually get to it, before moving on to the next task. It moved completely against how Eric saw life. Life was something to go for, directly and enthusiastically.

But for Minnie, if the task was emptying the trash (a larger task than you might think in such a large house), instead of just emptying the trash, she would water a plant or two near the trash and perhaps sit and invite Eric to look out the window at the heat shimmering on the lawn, or spend a few minutes moving a vase from one dresser to another. Eventually, slowly, she would take out the trash, and then perhaps sit again to glance at the paper afterward. It was a whole different way of thinking about the world.

At first, this drove Eric crazy. But after some time passed, he found himself falling into an odd state of mind—alert but tranquil. The leaves were slowly swirling outside like slow motion dust devils. The house began to take on a quality that was hard to describe: almost shimmery—timeless.

Of course, in retrospect the grandaunt was the meditation master trying to instruct her small nephew. When Eric reflected on all this many years later, he saw her profundity, which she had expressed, not with words, but through action itself. She, of course, never would have put it this way. She was just trying to civilize the boy a bit. And how was she doing it? By utilizing the time-honored practice of puttering. It is a skill not much in use today but one for which there is a great need.

Puttering is the state of letting your mind relax and becoming one with your environment. It is not a nervous energy but a relaxed unfolding. Something like a Japanese tea ceremony: it does not rely on concentration but on letting the moment define itself.

We often feel the need to put grand-sounding words on our activities, which really isn't necessary. Often the simplest thing is the best. Puttering is a little bit foreign to busy, hyper Americans. It's best to take it up slowly, a few minutes here and there; a few moments before the rush of the day begins, or after the day has begun to wind down. Be warned, however: puttering is not the same as vegging out in front of the TV. It is not mindlessness. Puttering is direction, but it is vague in its outline. Try it today. Choose a predetermined amount of time simply to putter in your favorite room. Puttering permits the mind to unhinge and simply absorb: simply to be. Practicing the art of puttering will prove invaluable as a steady exercise of the moment.

---

# A Moment to Do Nothing

From the outside looking in, you're productive and successful. So much so, in fact, that you most likely mask how stressed out or anxious you really are—maybe even from yourself. Objectively, no one would ever guess how overwhelmed or strung out you're feeling. For having a million and one things going on all the time, you keep it together pretty darn well, day after day.

The morning alarm sounds, you roll out of bed, stumble to the bathroom, wash, brush, primp, and welcome the start of a fresh day. You pull clothes from drawers—maybe yours and your children's—and quickly dress. Next, into the kitchen, where you chop, prepare, and pack food for the day. Before you know it, you're in the car, speeding along to morning appointments or to work just after you stop by the nearest coffee shop for a mandatory sustaining dose of caffeine.

To you, this behavior is normal. One event continues to pile on top of another that overlaps with yet another. The activity rarely if ever stops and, for the most part, you don't even realize that you may want it to.

But what if, just for a moment, you stopped juggling everything. Can you imagine how you would feel if you actually chose to stop doing anything for a brief period of time on a regular basis? Could you stand it? Would you be able to sit still?

Most people have little idea how to do nothing, well. Although in some countries doing nothing—or truly relaxing—is ingrained in the culture; it's expected. In Italy, for instance, everyone takes a siesta in the middle of the afternoon. A siesta is a period of time that lasts for about two hours every single day. During this time, businesses close and people go home to relax. They do this every single day; it's expected of them.

Admittedly, your life is full, but it doesn't have to be as busy as you make it. Everyone can stand to cut back on their activity, we just don't know how. The prescription for relief is to learn to stop. Even if you think you don't need to, try it. Try saying no to an invitation or an obligation. In the time you would have spent doing that activity, schedule time to do nothing at all. You can begin by doing nothing for just a couple of minutes a day. Eventually, you can try to gradually increase the amount of time you do nothing. For the greatest benefit, you'll learn to do nothing for a minimum of twenty minutes a day. But start with just two minutes. See if you can do that.

Rachel was the mother of two, and drove a minivan as if it were a racecar and cathedral all in one. Moving along at sixty-five miles per hour, she shared stories with her children, conducted interviews via her cell phone, ate lunch, listened to books on tape, and more, every day. There wasn't a second to spare. She even utilized the brief pause at stoplights to update her appointment book or write a quick note to prospective clients.

In one day, Rachel nursed her child's broken heart, fired an employee, discussed possibly going to counseling sessions with her partner, and consoled a distraught friend recently diagnosed with cancer. With forty minutes to spare, Rachel began racing the minivan toward the gym. If she could just squeeze in a thirty-minute workout, she could still arrive at her child's day care center on time. She felt fine, she thought. It's just been a full day.

Rushing toward the gym, Rachel's van stalled. Without missing a beat, she changed lanes and coasted to the side of the road. Turning off her ignition, she just sat still wondering what she should do. Her breath eased toward relaxation and before she knew what she was doing, Rachel caught herself doing nothing at all.

A sweet, delicious smile spread across her lips as she realized that doing nothing was exactly what she needed. Goodness. She did nothing for ten complete holy minutes, and then decided to spend the next five minutes scheduling "nothing moments" into her calendar. "Pull to side of road and do nothing," she wrote. Refreshed from her inaugural moment of nothingness, Rachel knew she had learned a valuable lesson. After vowing to regularly do nothing, Rachel turned the key in the ignition and, surprisingly, the minivan started right up.

Doing nothing is actually one of the most difficult activities to accomplish. Challenge yourself. See if you can do nothing at all some time today.

# Mindful Memories

It's no secret that when you spend time away from your daily routine, you gain perspective, increase your energy, and truly relax. When you're on vacation, for instance, you probably laugh more easily, worry less, and gain a grander, more accepting perception of your concerns back home.

It is much the same for any life-enhancing experience: attending outstanding theater, spending a day at an amusement park, hiking through a beautiful state park, playing an exhilarating game of ball, or tennis, or rugby. All these activities viscerally remind you of the sometimes all-too-fleeting joys and refreshment of your life. They rejuvenate your spirit, causing you to be more carefree and a lot more accepting and appreciative of your current situation, whatever it may be.

One way to expand your most energetic, rejuvenating moments is to create a *mindful memory* of them. With a little effort and intention, mindful memories will allow you to capture and extend the relaxation of your last vacation, the peacefulness you felt as you walked along the shore, the delight that overtook you during a theater experience, the exhilaration you experienced when your team won its last game, and more.

Creating a mindful memory is simple and effective. First, you must acquire an object that is symbolic of your experience. Whether it's a ball game, a jaunt through a rain forest, or a day out on a boat, locate or buy a tangible object that reminds you of the experience. Examples include natural objects such as rocks, tree branches, seashells, and manufactured memorabilia such as a tennis ball, a special piece of jewelry, a candleholder.

Once you acquire the object, set aside a few moments to mindfully create a feeling that will return you again and again to the essence of your experience. For example, if you've chosen a seashell as your object, hold the shell in your hand, examine its color, shape, and beauty, and then think of or say aloud what it is you are feeling in that moment: "I love breathing in the fresh air of the ocean. I feel good, hopeful, encouraged, and happy." Then, slip the object in your pocket or pack it away. Once you're home, place the object somewhere that you'll regularly see it. When your gaze crosses the path of your mindful memory, you'll be surprised just how swiftly you're reminded of the particular way you felt during your moment.

Dale had been a deep-sea diver since he was a child, and his home was filled with mindful memories. He had more memorable rocks and shells and other interesting sea objects than most beachside retail stores. Whether it was an exotic nautilus shell, an interesting sea sponge, or any of the other eye-catching objects he collected, a mere glance in their direction and Dale would recall in detail a delightful, sometimes adventuresome, and always affirming happening he had experienced.

During the summer, Dale traveled to the Bahamas to dive and swim with dolphins. The aqua blue of the water was so clear and vivid and calm that it was almost surreal. When he spotted and swam with a school of nearly twenty dolphins, his experience took on nearly prophetic meaning. For ten days, Dale dove and swam among some of the most inspiring, magnificent sea life he had ever seen.

Being the consummate mindful memory practitioner that he was, Dale brought home from the Bahamas a beautiful conch shell and also a bar of soap he bought in a small souvenir store. A month later, during a very rushed morning shower, Dale absentmindedly reached for the soap and almost immediately laughed aloud in joy and reverie. Sitting on the ledge was a plastic toy dolphin encased in the soap he'd bought in the Bahamas. Instantaneously, Dale gushed with the love and peace and wonder he had experienced on his dive with real, live dolphins.

Mindful memories are a simple and inexpensive way to extend your most precious memories. Whether it's a rock, bracelet, or postcard, or any other simple object, indulge in the sustainable art of mindful memories.

# Making the Most of a Moment

Day-to-day moments pass relatively quickly: seconds, hours, and days often fly by without your giving them another thought. When a sweetened moment penetrates your awareness—one that especially touches your heart or caresses your mind—it can be so fleeting that you barely remember it occurred at all. And yet, it is these delicious, sweetened moments of connection that add meaning to living.

Experiences of intimacy, connection, good will, interaction, and acute awareness of others create the meaning you need to sustain your day-to-day living. Even with a packed calendar and an ever growing to-do list, meaningful moments are continually occurring. Sometimes they require you to step out of your normal routines or comfort zone, but always they're right in front of you, waiting to be seized.

Jennifer was flying between Las Vegas and California, a trip she took at least three times a year to visit her folks. On this particular flight, clouds blanketed the horizon, obliterating all visual stimuli other than the puff of cumulus cotton. The woman next to Jennifer ordered an orange juice accompanied by a miniature bottle of vodka; Jennifer ordered a ginger ale. As the drinks arrived, Jennifer became lost momentarily in the gratitude she felt for the opportunity of flying safely, of being able to travel hundreds of miles in less than ninety minutes, of being healthy and happy, of knowing firsthand about true love.

"I propose a toast," Jennifer said aloud, surprised by the sound of her own voice penetrating her reverie.

The robust woman turned slowly toward Jennifer and smiled broadly, her drink poised in midair, "To what?"

"To life and love, to joy and prosperity," Jennifer said, just before touching her ginger ale to the woman's cup. They both leaned back in their seats contentedly.

Moments passed. Then, quietly, Jennifer heard her seatmate's voice, barely a whisper over the reverberating cabin noise: "If I could add anything," she said, "it would be health. Yes, to health."

The women smiled at each other and once again touched cup to cup. The moment passed, the woman returned to her reading material, and Jennifer gazed out the window. Just then, the jet dipped beneath the puffy white clouds and the most beautiful scene of the snow-capped mountains of Yosemite came into view through the window.

In that moment, Jennifer was aware of everything: the beauty outside, the forced air vent flirting with the hair against her cheek, the murmur of conversation behind her. She was deeply moved as another wave of gratitude profoundly flooded her being.

It's times like these, when connection and shared experience breeze into your present moment, that you're gently reminded of the sweet delicacy of living, of the opportunity to share your life with others, of the reality that being alive is an extraordinary gift.

It only takes a moment to shift into soulful awareness, a type of attentiveness that turns everyday moments into meaningful ones. And it doesn't require much effort: a simple moment of pause and acknowledgment will move you toward making the most of these moments.

Opportunities of soulful awareness present themselves every day:

- ❖ Smiling at another driver when you're both at a stop sign

- ❖ Paying for the car behind you as you pass through a toll, taking a moment to sincerely connect and say hello to the tollbooth operator

- ❖ Asking the grocery clerk how their day is and taking a moment to appreciate their answer

- ❖ Helping a neighbor move a heavy trash can to the corner of their driveway and commenting on how lovely their garden is

Making the time—just an extra pause in most cases—to turn the mundaneness of moments into meaning will add soulful distinction to your days. It's simply a matter of paying attention, taking an extra breath, and reveling in your life's momentous opportunities.

# Is This Body Me?

Everything in life is based in change. Even the mountains wear away. Most people tend to live life as if they themselves were permanent, even though they know, in truth, this idea is foolish. All of physical reality is based on the fact that nothing is static. This awareness can be exhilarating, but it can also be very frightening and depressing. How this awareness affects you depends on how impermanence reflects in you, in the mirror of your life.

Hannah had never felt the need to grow up so much as now. Living on her own at the university was unrelentingly adult, or at least far more adult than she was used to. People insisted on treating her differently, though exactly what the difference was she was having trouble putting her finger on. It seemed people on the street looked at and treated her differently than she was used to.

Hannah inspected herself in the full-length mirror that hung on the bedroom door of her room. Her roommate was out for the evening, which was just as well, because she needed to take some time with herself. Her face was very intent. She took a long time going over her body and her face, scrutinizing every part of herself. She was in no hurry. She was intensely curious—and troubled.

"Is this me?" she asked herself out loud. "Am I this body? Am I only this body? How is it that I am housed in this? It doesn't really feel like me. Am I different than this body? What is the connection? When people see me, is it me or something else they're seeing?" They were questions that had never really occurred to her before. But now, it was somehow different. At first she thought it was just gender and the continued flowering of puberty. But it seemed more than that, or was it?

She mused on in this vein for a long time, wondering and thinking if she could change the me that people saw by wearing different clothes and having exotic piercing and tattoos.

When Hannah's roommate came home, she was a little perplexed. "Whatcha doin'?"

"Trying to see me," Hannah replied.

"Uh huh. Any luck?"

And they proceeded to talk halfway through the night about it. Hannah was amazed that her roommate had experienced a similar feeling. "What do you do about it? Doesn't it feel weird, never knowing who it is another person is talking to? Doesn't it drive you crazy?" she asked.

Like for most of us, there was no final answer in their discussion; no final understanding. The process of individuality is an ongoing one: one that we work out again and again throughout our lives. It is defined by class, by gender, by age. Each definition and perception is real and yet strangely not, at the same time.

This fluidity is part of the consciousness that is our essence as a person. Our need to understand this process better within ourselves manifests as an ability to consciously take on various types of personas, and be, if for only a short time, someone else.

You can have a little fun with this reality by playing with appearances and noticing how others respond to you. For example, you can change your way of dressing. If you are normally very casual, become very formal. If very prim, become a vamp. Most of your friends and family will treat you just the same regardless of how you look, but acquaintances and strangers see only the persona you present (and they perceive). None of it is real, really. All of it is absolutely real. It is the act of constantly looking into the mirror and seeing a face. But whose face it is, finally, is the question we ask. Who is this body? Is this body you?

---

# The Surprise of Not Knowing

People yearn to develop and learn at a rapid pace. If they don't progress quickly enough, they become restless. Overall, this restlessness has stood people in good stead, but it has an expensive emotional price of making it difficult to find peace. Most often, the solution is a relentless drive to develop activities that only adds fuel to the flame.

When you don't understand something, for example, haven't you found yourself thinking that if you only read two or three more books or took another class, then you would have a firm grasp on the necessary information? Although this may be so in terms of book knowledge, the only understanding that ultimately satisfies and brings peace is inner understanding. Unfortunately, the straightforward acquisition of learning often is a barrier to inner knowing. Many people are addicted to knowledge and to the idea of knowing that it brings, but the result is intoxication, not harmony.

John was in the process of writing his dissertation—or at least trying to. But he couldn't seem to move forward in any significant way. Every day he would make new resolutions to move ahead. But the moment he wrote a paragraph or two, it occurred to him that he couldn't really write a single additional word without reading such and such new study that had just appeared, or ordering the transcript of a talk given by a scholar in the field of his topic, or, or, or. The list just kept getting longer. He knew it was getting crazy, but he felt helpless to stop. "A little more, a little more!" was his mantra. "If I just learn a little more, then I will know enough."

His girlfriend told him, "You can't know everything. Just go cold turkey," she said. "Just sit down and finish the thing. Good or bad, it will be finished." And he knew in his heart she was right, but still that voice kept saying: "One more book, one more article."

It is important for you to at least recognize the compulsion of "one more thing." It is a problem and an attitude that arises from consciousness, and many

114

people suffer from it. It resides in the belief that knowing just a little more will make a difference in your life—that understanding or health, or a relationship or wisdom can be achieved by just a little more of something. But the "something" always changes; it is never the same "something"—not for you—not for anyone else.

Very, very rarely is it the case that external learning will change your heart or attitude to any appreciable degree—not the amount of academic work you do, or even the success in your given profession, which is the culmination of the accumulation of knowledge.

For modern people, the clarity of deeper self must come not from the reading of libraries full of material, but from another direction. It must come from the deep affirmation and acceptance that *I*, the simple *I* of my day-to-day consciousness, does not know and can never know.

Accepting that you don't know and can never truly know much of anything, really, is a shock and a surprise. To know and accept this as accurate, however, is to truly embrace yourself and your life. There is no such thing as "personal evolution," per se. There is the cold water of existence splashing in your face, which can be difficult to accept. Yet, anything that helps you wake up to this truth is beneficial.

A great person once said, "Live frugally on surprise. Expect nothing." Try to live your life this way. To keep this intention in mind, you can write on the back of your hand or on a Post-It note: "I do not know what will happen today." Throughout the day, refer to it; remind yourself that you truly know very little, if anything at all. Let the day unfold itself and whatever happens, experience it as a surprise.

Not knowing is the highest state of the mind. Not knowing what tomorrow will bring. Not knowing if this will be a day of rain or sun. Not knowing any final truth, or even some of the more minor ones! Not knowing is the state in which all true creation arises. For the world is perfect and its surprises always are awe filled. The sense of "knowing" is what creates the obstacles.

---

# Seeking Answers, Finding Your Purpose

Randy was troubled. His closest friends—all, like Randy, in their mid-thirties—were reaching a point in their lives where they seemed to have found their purpose. Carrie had cast aside an unfulfilling job in favor of a career where she could help others. Jane and Kelvin, who had struggled with fertility problems, were now the proud parents of healthy twins. Randy was happy for them, but he couldn't help feeling that the kind of joy they were experiencing would never happen to him. His own life was fine; in fact, it was pretty much as he'd always imagined it would be. But there was nothing in particular that made him light up and burn with passion.

Even in his spiritual life, Randy felt he was missing out on some secret, some mystery. People had been talking about a "higher power" for as long as he could remember. But Randy was having doubts whether there was even such a thing. The truth was, he realized, people had been arguing about such things for ages.

The more he thought about it, the more he realized that in the final analysis there is no way to prove the existence of anything because no proof can ever be proof enough. Nothing anyone can say, no rational explanation, no syllogism can ever be enough for anything that is of fundamental importance to a person. The changes Randy had witnessed in his friends worked in the same way. He knew plenty of other people who were perfectly content with their lives. But Carrie, Jane, and Kelvin weren't just happier than they had been before—they were transformed, radiant with purpose and fulfillment. Some other kind of force was at work, something that couldn't be defined.

Randy thought about it further: If a person is convinced that no part of existence houses a divine spirit or comes from a divine source—then no mere word can possibly change their mind. These questions are not a matter of argument, but experience. This realization came to Randy like an electric wire of understanding zapping straight into his heart. And everything changed. He remembered a parable told to him years ago—he couldn't even recall by whom, but it had stuck with him.

It went as follows: Once there was a little girl made of salt. One morning she woke up asking, "What is my purpose?" She tried to put the question out of her mind, but it kept rising up. It was like an itch that had to be scratched. Soon, she started asking other creatures if they knew her purpose. She traveled a long distance. But regardless of whom she met, when she asked them her question, they were stumped. Neither the chipmunk nor the sage could tell her anything that was satisfactory.

At last, out of patience and ready to give up, she came to a great ocean. She was about to ask the ocean her question, but before she could, she noticed that the ocean was singing to her. It was calling with such a beautiful and inviting song. She stepped forward and put her foot into the water. Immediately she felt its tug and its power, and it was like she had found something she lost long ago. She took another step and another. A voice whispered in her heart, "It was for this you were created. This is your home."

The experience of the divine is a total experience. Sometimes we are afraid of having total experiences because when we do, the little *I* is extinguished. When we have the experience of truly letting go, boundaries of the mind are released. The heart becomes a sky without limit. Spaciousness. Surrender feels like a risk. This risk, however, is always worthwhile, because after the surrender, you are filled with the spaciousness of true balance and the relief of profound purpose.

Think about your past. Can you pinpoint times when you retreated from the divine ocean of faith, rather than surrendering? What stopped you? Did you even realize at the time that you were fearful of what might happen if you allowed yourself to be transformed? After you've considered an example or two from your life, consider how your life might be different had you been guided less by security and more by the divine directions in front of you.

The next time you feel tugged toward the source, surrender to it; trust that it's the most direct route to purpose.

**Jueli Gastwirth** has studied various forms of spiritual practice and body centered therapies with nationally renowned teachers. She currently lives in the San Francisco Bay Area.

**Avram Davis, Ph.D.**, is founder and codirector of Chochmat HaLev, the only independent center for Jewish meditation in the country. The teachings of Chochmat HaLev are based within the Jewish mystical tradition. He teaches extensively across the United States, including weekend and weeklong workshops, seminars, and retreats.

# Some Other New Harbinger Titles

*The Daughter-In-Law's Survival Guide*, Item DSG $12.95

*PMDD*, Item PMDD $13.95

*The Vulvodynia Survival Guide*, Item VSG $15.95

*Love Tune-Ups*, Item LTU $10.95

*The Deepest Blue*, Item DPSB $13.95

*The 50 Best Ways to Simplify Your Life*, Item FWSL $11.95

*Brave New You*, Item BVNY $13.95

*Loving Your Teenage Daughter*, Item LYTD $14.95

*The Hidden Feelings of Motherhood*, Item HFM $14.95

*The Woman's Book of Sleep*, Item WBS $14.95

*Pregnancy Stories*, Item PS $14.95

*The Women's Guide to Total Self-Esteem*, Item WGTS $13.95

*Thinking Pregnant*, Item TKPG $13.95

*The Conscious Bride*, Item CB $12.95

*Juicy Tomatoes*, Item JTOM $13.95

*Facing 30*, Item F30 $12.95

*The Money Mystique*, Item MYST $13.95

*High on Stress*, Item HOS $13.95

*Perimenopause, 2nd edition*, Item PER2 $16.95

*The Infertility Survival Guide*, Item ISG $16.95

*After the Breakup*, ATB $13.95

Call **toll free, 1-800-748-6273,** or log on to our online bookstore at **www.newharbinger.com** to order. Have your Visa or Mastercard number ready. Or send a check for the titles you want to New Harbinger Publications, Inc., 5674 Shattuck Ave., Oakland, CA 94609. Include $4.50 for the first book and 75¢ for each additional book, to cover shipping and handling. (California residents please include appropriate sales tax.) Allow two to five weeks for delivery.

*Prices subject to change without notice.*